the modern embroidery handbook

Learn over 70 hand embroidery stitches step-by-step,
plus 20 colourful projects and a sampler

I made this hoop for my little rainbow, Alfie, the sweetest soul who always sees the best in everything. This book is for you, Alfie - I love you so much.

the modern embroidery handbook

Learn over 70 hand embroidery stitches step-by-step, plus 20 colourful projects and a sampler

CLARE ALBANS

Photographs by Jesse Wild and Clare Albans

WHITE OWL

For Alfie
Always look for rainbows

First published in Great Britain in 2024 and reprinted in 2025 by
PEN & SWORD WHITE OWL
An imprint of Pen & Sword Books Ltd
Yorkshire – Philadelphia

www.hellohooray.com @hellohoorayblog

ISBN 978-1-39904-132-4

A CIP catalogue record for this book is available from the British Library.

Group Publisher: Jonathan Wright
Series Editor and Publishing Consultant: Katherine Raderecht
Art Director: Jane Toft
Editor and stylist: Katherine Raderecht
Photography: Jesse Wild and Clare Albans
Nails: Cheryl at Totally Polished Hair; Susan Mason at The Hair Cabin

The Publisher's authorised representative in the EU for product safety is Authorised Rep Compliance Ltd., Ground Floor, 71 Lower Baggot Street, Dublin D02 P593, Ireland.
www.arccompliance.com

For a complete list of Pen & Sword titles please contact:

PEN & SWORD BOOKS LIMITED
47 Church Street, Barnsley, South Yorkshire S70 2AS, England
E-mail: enquiries@pen-and-sword.co.uk
Website: www.pen-and-sword.co.uk
or
PEN AND SWORD BOOKS
1950 Lawrence Rd, Havertown, PA 19083, USA
E-mail: Uspen-and-sword@casematepublishers.com
Website: www.penandswordbooks.com

contents

introduction

In Autumn 2020, I was eagerly awaiting the release of my first book, Colourful Fun Embroidery. After a strange year of Covid lockdowns, it was wonderful to finally hold a copy in my hands! However, it coincided with me going through a bit of a creative rut. I wasn't sure how long it would last and was beginning to wonder if I'd ever have an idea for a new project again! Then I remembered that when I started blogging, it was trying something new that sparked my creativity. I suddenly felt energised and excited. I wanted to give myself a period of exploration to help me get my mojo back.

In 2021, I decided to teach myself a new embroidery stitch every week and share my learning experience on YouTube. The Happy Stitch Project was born! I started with the five stitches I knew and, by the end of the year, I had learned a new stitch every week without fail and my creative mojo had returned. The project changed and adapted along the way, which was a true reflection of the creative process, and a huge bonus was the joy of seeing people joining in every week.

The Modern Embroidery Handbook brings together everything I learned about hand embroidery through my self-taught Happy Stitch Project. Use the book to get started on your hand embroidery journey or to experiment further if you know the basics already. I've included a few stitches that are new to me here too (in keeping with the spirit of the original project) so even if you joined in with The Happy Stitch Project, there's more to learn.

The book builds on the idea of traditional stitch guides from the past, and gives you step-by-step instructions on how to do 72 different stitches. There are also 20 projects, plus a sampler to try all the stitches. I have divided the book into six chapters. The first chapter of the book introduces you to the sampler project, and there are then four chapters of stitches and projects: First Stitches, Borders and Edging, Decorative Stitches and Motifs, and Textures and Knots. In the final chapter you'll find useful links and project templates. Please note that thread colours used throughout are DMC shades.

I hope this book inspires you to try embroidery for the first time, or to get out of your comfort zone and try something new if you are a more experienced stitcher. I hope it gives you the confidence to make mistakes and to be bold in trying new things, and that you refer to it time and again. Most of all, I hope this book brings you joy in taking time out to be creative.

chapter 1: the sampler

I absolutely love embroidery samplers. The combination of different designs, colours and techniques brought to life through this simple but effective medium is amazing. What I love the most is that they are such personal pieces, showing the stitches and techniques that an individual has learned to craft over time. A sampler is a bit like keeping a journal through stitching; each stitch telling a story. This sampler will tell your story.

Sampler materials

- 35cm (14") quilting or embroidery hoop to stitch in (not essential, but recommended)
- 30cm (12") quilting or embroidery hoop to display in
- Essex linen in white - a 45 x 45cm (roughly 18 x 18") piece will fit both hoop sizes
- A water erasable pen
- A ruler to trace the design
- Thread - light red (3705), dark orange (740), light tangerine (742), yellow (726), bright green (907), teal (3851), light kingfisher (996), kingfisher (995), light purple (340), bright purple (333), magenta (917), light pink (604)
- Some white perle thread to finish the back

Setting up the sampler hoop

Transfer the design (template on page 118) onto your fabric using a water erasable pen. Take your time and use a long ruler for the straight edges. Don't worry if you make a mistake - the pen will come out later.

Place the fabric in the larger hoop to stitch. Check the tension of the fabric. You want to aim for something resembling a drum skin. Keep checking and adjusting the tension if necessary as you stitch.

Rather than outline each section as you go along, it is much easier to stitch them all first. Using three strands of thread, make small backstitches to outline each section.

Stitching the sampler

The stitch tutorials for all 72 stitches on the sampler appear in the chapters that follow. The step-by-step photos show you how to make the stitch. To help you position your stitches in the right place on the sampler, each stitch is numbered. Simply use the handy stitch guide on the following page. The template is in Chapter 6 or you can download a digital version by scanning the QR code on page 118. You can do your stitches in any order, but it's helpful to stitch any that meet the edges of the smaller hoop in the larger 14" hoop first before transferring to the smaller display hoop.

The full template is in the final chapter at the back of the book, or you can download a digital version by scanning the QR code on page 118.

stitch guide

In this stitch guide and on the sampler image on the opposite page are all 72 embroidery stitches included in the 20 projects and on the sampler in this book. Whilst I have grouped the stitches into four different chapters in the book, this is by no means exclusive. The great thing about hand embroidery is that you can use the stitches in lots of different ways. For example, a stitch from textures and knots might also look great in part of a pattern for a border too. So feel free to experiment!

FIRST STITCHES (PAGES 12-15)

These stitches are so wonderfully versatile and, because of this, you'll find them in most embroidery patterns - from those for beginners right up to ones for more advanced stitchers.

1 Straight 2 Backstitch 3 Satin 4 Link/lazy daisy 5 French knot 6 Fern 7 Seeding 8 Stem 9 Star 10 Chain 11 Fly 12 Running

BORDERS & EDGING (PAGES 35-43)

These stitches are generally used for borders and edging because they work really well along straight or curved lines. However, many of them are also brilliant for text or little decorative touches too, so get creative with how you use them in your stitching.

13 Cable 14 Whipped backstitch 15 Scroll 16 Cretan 17 Coral 18 Rope 19 Blanket 20 Whipped running 21 Couching 22 Split 23 Laced running 24 Bosnian 25 Closed buttonhole 26 Buttonhole 27 Chevron 28 Twisted chain 29 Petal 30 Chained feather 31 Herringbone 32 Zig zag chain

DECORATIVE STITCHING & MOTIFS (PAGES 64-71)

Many embroidery stitches create their own little motif, so they're perfect for individual elements in a design. You can also stitch them in repeat patterns for a different effect.

33 Woven cross 34 Long-tail daisy 35 Tulip 36 Brick and Cross 37 Arrowhead 38 Feather 39 Eyelet 40 Pistil 41 Thorn 42 Sheaf 43 Scallop 44 Leaf 45 Ermine 46 Double fern 47 Buttonhole wheel 48 Whipped wheel 49 Woven star 50 Open chain 51 Closed feather 52 Zig zag

TEXTURES & KNOTS (PAGES 91-97)

Many of the stitches in this chapter are considered more advanced than in the other chapters. The main reason is that they often take a little more practice to get the tension just right, but I promise you that they're worth the effort!

53 Woven wheel 54 Danish knot 55 Square boss 56 Bullion knot 57 Long and short 58 Padded satin 59 Turkey 60 Palestrina 61 Colonial knot 62 Ring knot 63 Loop 64 Cast on 65 Forbidden 66 Fishbone 67 Brick 68 Crown 69 Pearl 70 Satin couching 71 Trellis 72 Weave

chapter 2: first stitches

This chapter includes stitches commonly used in embroidery kits and patterns. You could call them 'basic stitches', but I wanted to avoid that word because one person's 'basic' stitch can be another person's nemesis! If you're a beginner, you may find some of these a little fiddly at first but just be patient with yourself.

Before we start, it's going to be helpful to explain the terms 'stabbing method' and 'sewing method'. The 'stabbing method' is when you come up through your fabric and then take it back through again to make each stitch. The 'sewing method' is where you come up through the fabric, and the needle stays on the surface for stitching. I've indicated where to use the sewing method; otherwise use the stabbing method.

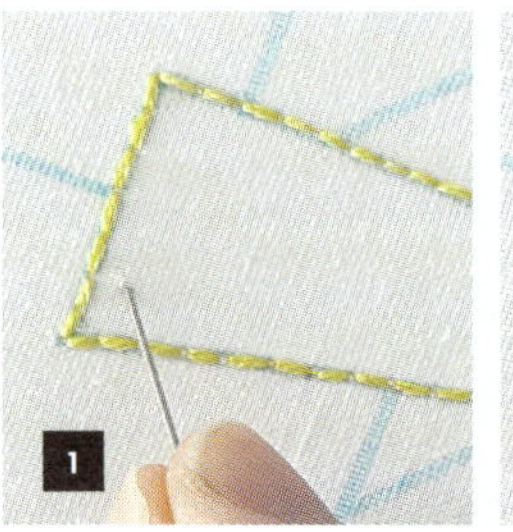

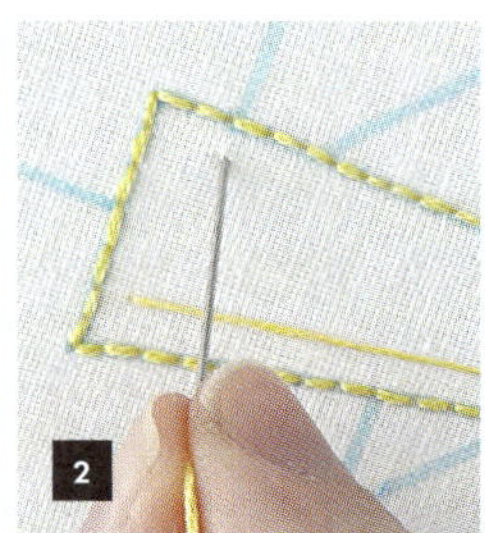

Straight (1)
1. Bring the needle up through the fabric, and push it back through to create your desired stitch length.
2. Repeat as required.

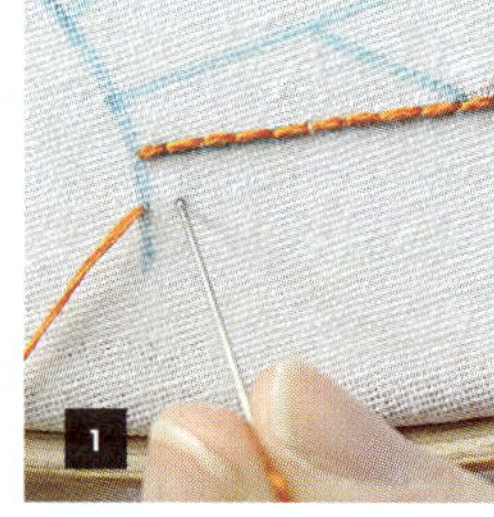

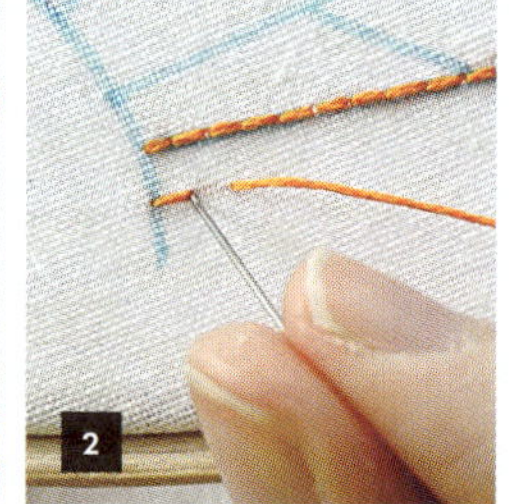

Backstitch (2)
1. Come up through the fabric and push it back through to create a short straight stitch.
2. Then come back through the fabric a little further along the line to be stitched, leaving a gap the same size as the first stitch. Push the needle back through at the exact point where the first stitch ended. Repeat as required.

Satin (3)
1. Come up through the fabric and stitch a single horizontal straight stitch. Repeat, leaving a small gap between the stitches.

2. Repeat, leaving gaps between stitches and filling in with more stitches. Stitch a small area and fill, rather than spreading the stitches across the whole space.

Link/Lazy daisy (4)

1. Come up through the fabric, and push your needle back through as close as possible to where you came up. Leave a loop of thread on the top of the fabric.

2. Bring the needle back up through the loop, and pull gently so that it catches. Secure the stitch in place with a small anchor stitch over the bottom of the loop.

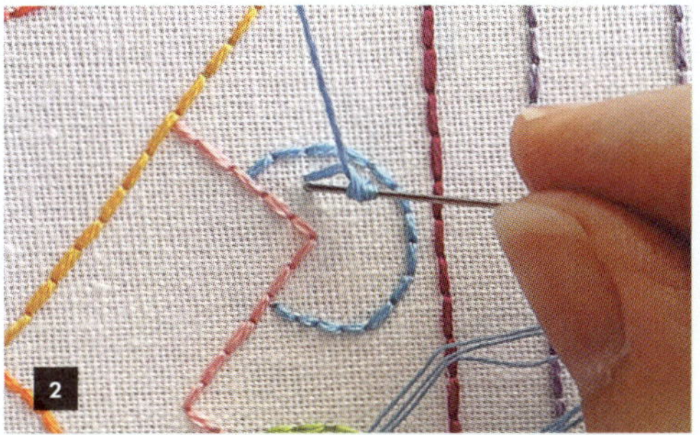

French knot (5)

1. Come up through the fabric. Hold the needle in front of the working thread and wrap it over the needle towards you, and back up to the top. Repeat twice more so that you have wrapped three times in total.

2. Put the needle back through the fabric, as close as possible to where it came out. Gently pull the working thread so it comes together around the bottom of the needle, before pulling through to create the knot.

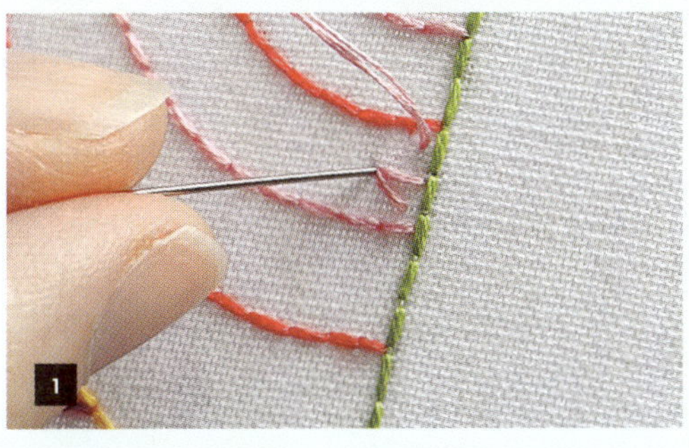

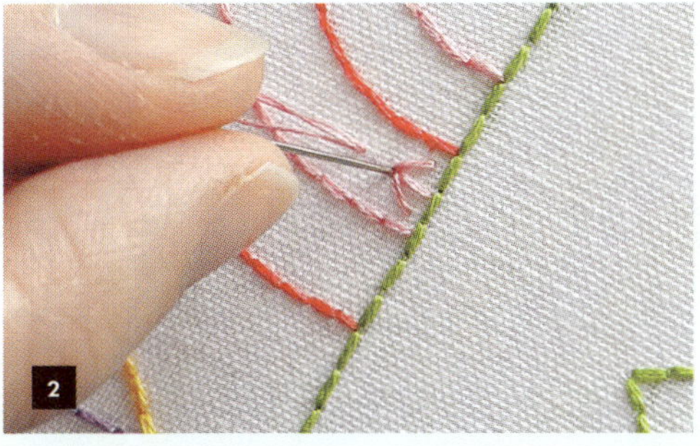

Fern (6)

1. Come up through the fabric, and stitch a single horizontal straight stitch. Come back up a little way above, and join it to where the first stitch ended to create a diagonal line. Repeat on the other side.

2. Stitch another horizontal stitch as before, joining it to the first as you would if stitching a backstitch. Add the diagonal stitches and repeat as required.

Seeding (7)

1. Stitch two small straight stitches with a small gap between them. Keep each stitch the same length.

2. Repeat, stitching another pair fairly close to the first but at a different angle. Continue until the whole area is covered.

Stem (8)

1. Come up through the fabric and create a small straight stitch. Come back up over the top in the centre as shown, without splitting it.

2. Push the needle back through the fabric to make a small stitch the same as the first stitch. Repeat as required.

Star (9)

1. Stitch a vertical straight stitch and then another central horizontal stitch the same size over the top. Add diagonal stitches, keeping these the same size.

2. Stitch smaller diagonal stitches over the centre, where the first stitches meet. Work in the gaps next to the vertical stitch.

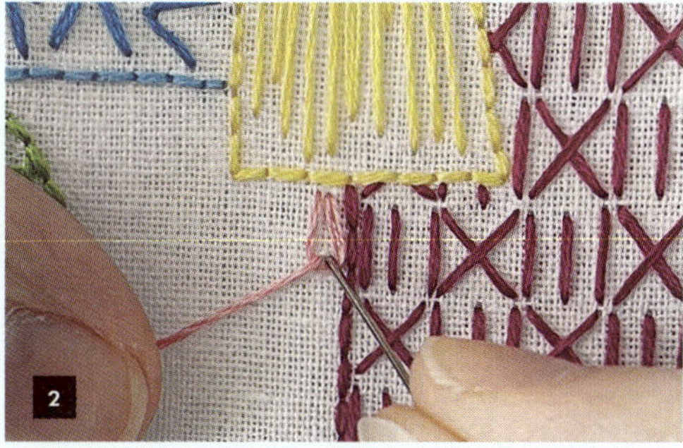

Chain (10)

1. Come up through the fabric, and push your needle back through as close as possible to where you came up. Leave a loop of thread on top of the fabric. Come back up at the bottom of the loop, and gently pull the thread through.

2. Push the needle back through again to create a second loop below the first. Repeat as required, securing the final loop with a small anchor stitch.

Fly (11)

1. Come up through the fabric and move the needle a little way to the right. Use the sewing method to bring the needle back up further down and centrally to the top of the stitch. Move the working thread under the needle.

2. Pull through and secure with a small anchor stitch at the bottom.

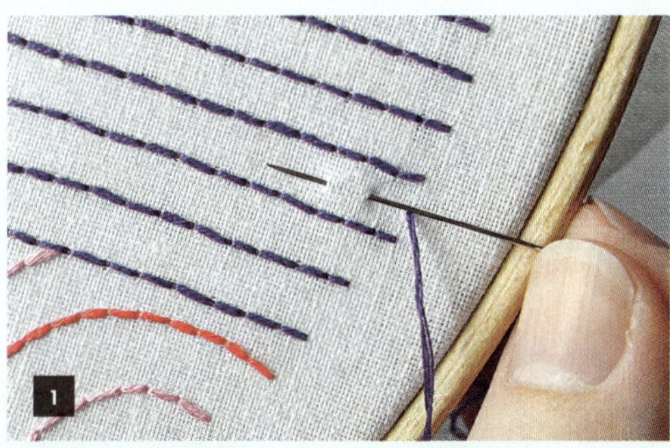

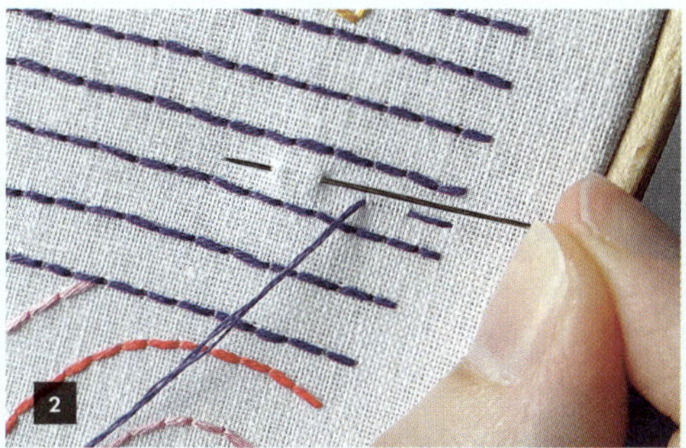

Running (12)

1. Bring the needle up through the fabric at the end of the line to be stitched. Using the sewing method, bring the needle down and up through the fabric, leaving a gap the same size as the first stitch.

2. Pull the needle through, and repeat as required.

cat nap hoop

Stitching a child's drawing is a really special project, and your little ones will love seeing their designs brought to life through embroidery.

Stitches: backstitch (with optional whipped backstitch), lazy daisy, straight, French knots, fly, fern.

You will need

- A 12cm (5") embroidery hoop
- 22 x 22cm (9 x 9") piece of green fabric
- A heat erasable pen, such as a Frixion pen
- Thread - light camel (977), camel (976), light green (164), mid green (989), mid forest green (988), mid purple (30), aubergine (32), lemon (445), off-white (3865)
- Perle No.8 thread in shade 3326 (pale pink) and 602 (dark pink)

Both our children love to draw and it's a huge part of their home education. Our daughter has recently discovered drawing tutorials online, and this sleeping cat was the first one she undertook. I stitched it onto a t-shirt for her and she was delighted - but she was even more thrilled when I asked if I could use it as part of a design for this book! When stitching a child's drawing, you can either stitch a full design, or use your own doodles around the drawing as I've done with the flowers here.

INSTRUCTIONS

1. Carefully trace the design onto the fabric using a heat erasable pen. Then place the fabric in your hoop.Using two strands of light camel thread (977), stitch small backstitches around the outline of the cat, and add the details on the paws and whiskers using straight stitches in the same colour. Use camel thread (976) to add the facial features with small backstitches too. I decided to whip backstitch the outline of the cat. Instructions are on page 35.

2

3

4

5

2. Stitch the tall stems either side of the cat with long straight stitches using 2 strands of mid forest green (988). The remaining grassy stitches are stitched using 2 strands of light green (164) and mid green (989), and you can stitch these colours randomly to give a natural grassy effect. I used the light green (164) for the stems of the dandelions.

3. Stitch the straight stitch flowers to the right of the cat using 3 strands of mid purple (30) and aubergine (32) thread. Use the darker shade for the petals at the bottom of the flowers and the lighter shade at the top, as this gives a natural effect. Add a French knot in the centre of each flower in lemon thread (445). Use fern stitch to add the plant detail next to the purple flowers.

Use 3 strands of mid green thread (989), starting from the top of the plant.

4. The little dandelions are stitched with 2 strands of off-white thread (3865), using a very small fly stitch. You could always use 1 strand for this if you prefer, but 2 strands joins each stitch together a little more to give the effect of the seeds.

5. Stitch the lazy daisies using light and dark pink perle thread. Once this is complete, you can carefully remove any visible pen marks by giving the hoop a quick blast with a hairdryer. I prefer this method to using an iron, as it doesn't flatten the stitches. If you wish, place the design in a painted hoop and then finish the back.

doodle shoes

As you start to feel more confident, it's great to get out of using embroidery hoops and stitch on something a bit less traditional - like these canvas shoes.

Stitches: backstitch.

You will need

- A pair of canvas shoes
- A water erasable pen (plus brush pen to remove it)
- Thread - light purple (340), light teal (964), dark pink (600) - use more or less colours if you prefer
- Some sharp needles
- A few pins (optional but really useful)
- A thimble (optional)

I'd wanted to try stitching on canvas shoes for ages, but heard that they can be hard to stitch on. The side sections are actually pretty easy on this type of canvas trainer, but the tricky section is the back of the heel because of the less flexible fabric in this area. You might want to invest in a thimble to help you push the needle through the fabric. Don't let this put you off - it's a fabulous project that will create shoes that are totally unique to you.

1

INSTRUCTIONS

1. Remove the laces from one of the shoes. Use an erasable pen to start doodling on the shoe. Start at the heel and draw a curved line that follows the semi-circular edge of the heel support. Draw two more lines within this section following the same line. As this section is the trickiest to stitch, it's best to keep the design simple here.

2

3

4

5

2. Continue to doodle over the shoe until it is completely covered. Draw different lines and shapes, filling them in with smaller versions of the same line or shape. You can draw as many as you like - just make it your own unique design. Remember that the pen marks will come out if you don't like the design and you can always stitch it slightly differently if you change your mind as you work on your shoe.

3. Choose a colour to start (I used light purple, 340) and thread a needle with three strands. Stitch regular sized backstitches over one of the lines. Repeat using the other colours you have chosen until the lines on the inner and outer sides of the shoe are stitched.

4. When it comes to stitching the heel of the shoe, it's quite helpful to use a pin to make small holes along the line to aid stitching. Please take extra care when doing this to mind your fingers! Push the pin from the outside to the inside of the shoe, and bring the needle through the hole from the inside each time.

5. When the first shoe is complete, repeat the previous steps with the second shoe. I tried to roughly copy the same design on the second shoe, but you don't need to do this if you don't want them to match. When stitching is complete, remove any visible pen lines. Put the laces back in and they're ready to wear.

You can find these canvas shoes in shops all over the high street in lots of different colours. They come in adult and children's sizes so your whole family can have a pair.

LOVE
YOUR
SELF

love yourself tee

It's so easy to embroider on a basic t-shirt, and you can easily customise this wardrobe staple with your favourite colours to compliment your existing outfits.

Stitches: backstitch, satin stitch.

You will need

- A pre-ironed plain white t-shirt
- A sheet of water soluble fabric stabiliser (such as Sulky Sticky Fabri-Solvy or DMC Magic Paper)
- An extra fine water erasable pen
- 12cm (5") embroidery hoop
- Thread - light pale yellow (745), mid beige (739), light terracotta (758), rose pink (760), pale lilac (26), light aubergine (28)

Water soluble fabric stabiliser enables you to stitch on tricky, stretchy fabrics. I use a water erasable pen to trace the design; the lines will disappear in the wash once you've finished stitching. Be careful with your choice of threads - DMC threads are colour-fast so I'd highly recommend using them; it would be sad if the colours ran after all your hard work. If you're stitching this project over a few days, remove the hoop before putting it down to avoid stretching the fabric. Just pop it back in when you start stitching again.

INSTRUCTIONS

1. Trace the design onto the stabiliser and cut around it, leaving roughly 1.5cm around each edge. Work out where you want the words to be stitched, and then peel off the backing paper and stick it onto the t-shirt. Place the inner ring of your hoop inside the t-shirt, position it around the design, place the outer hoop on top and tighten gently. Make sure that you only have the front of the t-shirt in the hoop, and that you haven't pulled it out of shape.

2. Thread a needle with 3 strands of the light pale yellow thread (745), and stitch around the edges of the letter with small backstitches. Using the same colour (and same number of strands), stitch the shadow of the letter using satin stitch. The satin stitches should diagonally follow the direction of the shadow of the lettering.

3. Repeat this process with the next letter, using 3 strands of mid beige thread (739). The curved edges of the middle of the letter are also stitched using backstitch. The middle should be completely stitched with a satin stitch following the direction of the shadow along the outer edge.

4. Continue stitching the letters in this way, with a different colour for each letter. I used the colours in the order in which they are listed on the materials list, repeating the list from the letter 'U' onwards.

5. Run a warm bowl of clean water and place the t-shirt in it to remove the stabiliser. I usually find that I need to run a garment through the washing machine to completely get rid of the residue from the stabiliser. Once dry, give the t-shirt a press around the stitching (but not over it) and then it's ready to wear.

LOVE
YOUR
SELF

stardust hoop

If you have a bit of experience of hand embroidery but still don't feel confident about designing your own patterns, this project will give you the freedom to experiment.

Stitches: satin, fern, straight, seeding, backstitch, French knot, star, chain, running.

You will need

- 15cm (6") embroidery hoop
- 22 x 22cm (9" x 9") piece of fabric in your chosen design
- Thread to match your fabric - dark orange (720), medium tangerine (741), light gold (18), mid deep water green (992), dark green (505), light blue (3325), mid rose pink (3688), off-white (3865).

Quilting cottons are brilliant for hand embroidery projects, because they come in so many different patterns and colours. Often we use the pattern on a fabric as a background for something else to be stitched on top, but you can use embroidery to embellish the pattern and emphasise particular elements of a fabric's design. Stitching over patterned fabric is a really simple way to practise new stitches. The beauty of this project is that we'll all make different versions, depending on the fabric you use and the position of the hoop.

1

INSTRUCTIONS

1. Position the fabric in your hoop. Look carefully at the print and see which section of the pattern you'd like to feature - here I chose to have the moon and stars fairly central but slightly off centre. Choose a section to start, and thread your needle with 3 strands of the matching thread. In this large section above the stars, I stitched vertical satin stitches to cover the whole section using mid deep water green thread (992).

2. Fern stitch works brilliantly for curved edges, and I've used it on this scalloped section here. Work with the curves as you go, keeping the central stitches running down the middle of the section as a guide to where to stitch the diagonal lines. Here, I've used three strands of mid rose pink thread (3688).

3. Straight stitches are also great for filling in curved sections. Here stitching them vertically along this section gives a sense of movement. Stitch each one at regular intervals, making sure that the stitches go right to either side of the pattern.

4. Add seeding stitches to fill different sections of the design. Here I used light blue thread (3325), and stitched the seeding stitches in groups of two. Then I added texture to the crescent moon by covering it with small, horizontal satin stitches in off-white thread (3865). I stitched star stitches over three of the largest stars using the same colour thread.

5. Choose a section to fill completely with French knots - I've used off-white thread (3865) to give the effect of a cloud. The final stitches to add are backstitch, running stitch and chain stitch, which make great outlines. Leave some areas of the pattern free from stitching so that the design can still be seen. Once complete, finish the back of the hoop so it's ready to display.

You can't pour
from an empty cup

cuppa hoop

This hoop combines my love of stitching with my love of tea, and it's also a reminder that it's always okay to take time out for self care.

Stitches: stem stitch, backstitch, seeding stitch.

You will need

- 20cm (8″) embroidery hoop
- A piece of pink fabric, roughly 31 x 31cm (12 x 12″)
- Thread - dark pink (601)
- Water erasable pen with a fine tip
- Brush pen
- No.8 perle thread in DMC 3326 to finish the back

I've always had to work hard to take time out for myself, and when I was designing this project I knew that 'you can't pour from an empty cup' were the perfect words to add to my design. The process of stitching the hoop really helped me to break through some mental barriers with making progress on this book. I stitched it during a particularly stressful time so it means a lot to me. I hope that while you are stitching this project, you will find it peaceful as well as a comforting reminder to look after yourself. While stitching this hoop, make sure you have a nice big pot of tea and a tin of your favourite teatime biscuits by your side!

1

2

INSTRUCTIONS

1. Carefully transfer the design onto the fabric using a fine tip water erasable pen (or a heat erasable one if you prefer). Thread your needle with two strands of dark pink thread (601). Start by stitching the hands with a very small stem stitch, keeping the stitches as evenly-sized as you can.

2. Once the hands are completed, thread your needle with another two strands of thread. Stitch the edges of the cup with small backstitches, keeping them as evenly sized as you can as you did when stitching the stem stitch.

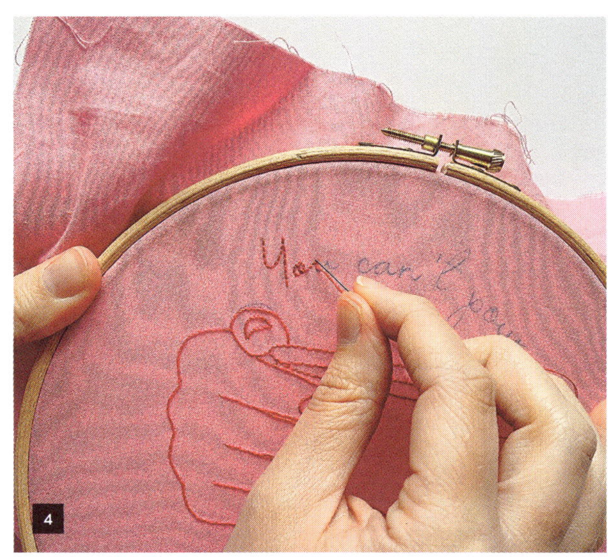

3. Add the line of tea in the cup using backstitch, but make these stitches slightly bigger to give a little more definition against the cup and hands.

4. Stitch the lettering using two strands of thread, and very small backstitches. The key to stitching hand lettering like this is to make sure you always stitch in the direction of the letters, as though you were writing the words. Try to tie off at the back between each word or where there is a gap in the lettering, so that you won't see any stray thread through the front of the fabric.

5. Thread a needle with one strand of the pink thread, and stitch tiny, single seeding stitches to give the tea some definition in the cup. Fill in the space by stitching them in different directions until this section is full. Remove any visible pen lines before finishing the back of your hoop.

chapter 3: borders and edging

'Borders and edging' pretty much sums up what these stitches are traditionally used for - but not entirely! Some of these stitches are amazing for lettering too, as well as patterns, filling stitches and so much more. There are some really fun projects in this section that will get you out of an embroidery hoop if you're feeling a little more adventurous. You can get really creative with how you use these stitches, and in the project section I'll give you a few ideas to get you started.

Cable (13)

1. Stitch a straight stitch at the end of the line. Come back up underneath the middle of the first stitch, making sure there isn't a gap and make a second stitch the same size.making this second stitch the same size as the first.

2. Make the third stitch by bringing the needle back up through the fabric where the first stitch ended, and make this next stitch as before. Repeat as required.

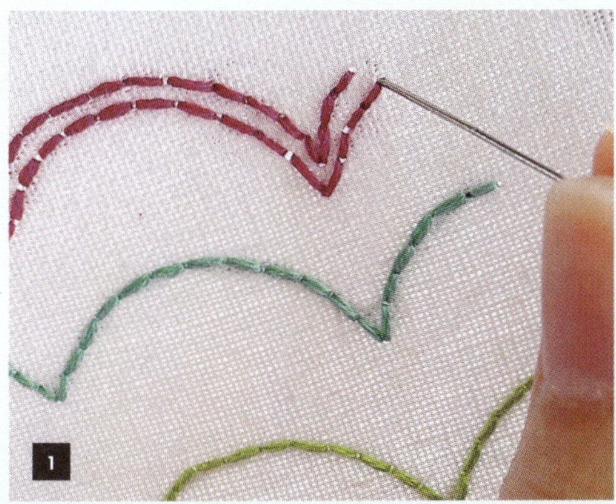

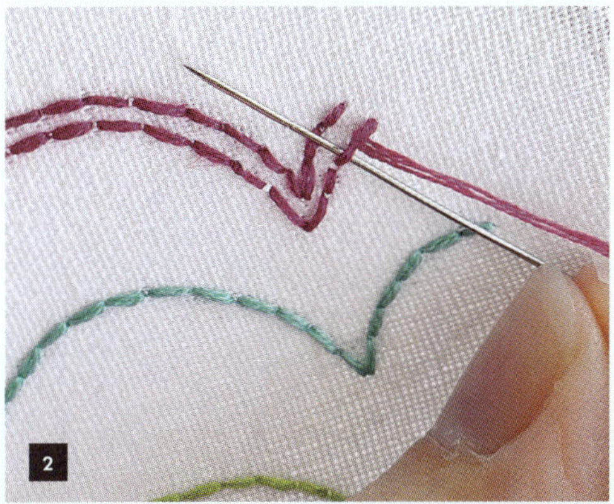

Whipped backstitch (14)

1. Stitch a line of backstitches. At the end of the line, come back up through the hole at the end of the last stitch.

2. Push the needle underneath the first stitch on top of the fabric. Repeat with the remaining stitches, working from the same side each time.

Scroll (15)

1. Come up through the end of the line (either draw one or just imagine there is one there). Use the sewing method to take your needle down just above and back up just below the line. Wrap the working thread around the back of the needle and around the bottom. Don't pull it too tightly here.

2. Gently pull the needle through the loop until a small knot is created. Repeat the steps above until you reach the end of the line. Finish on a straight stitch without a knot to balance the pattern.

Cretan (16)

1. Draw two horizontal lines onto the fabric with an erasable pen. Come up just above the bottom line as shown, and then take it diagonally to the top line using the sewing method. Push the needle down through the fabric just above this top line, and come up directly underneath it. Pull the needle through, making sure that the needle passes over the working thread.

2. Moving diagonally to the right, push the needle down through the fabric below the bottom line and come up just above the top of it. Move the working thread diagonally, before pulling the needle gently through again to create the next stitch. Repeat.

Coral (17)

1. Draw or imagine a straight line on the fabric. A little way along, use the sewing method to go through the fabric just above this line and come out just below it. Wrap the working thread over the top of the pointed end, and move the thread in the direction of the stitching, pulling the needle through.

2. Pull the working thread gently in the direction of the stitching to form the knot. Continue along the line in this way, making the knots evenly spaced.

Rope (18)

1. Come up through the fabric at the end of the line to be stitched. Use the sewing method to take your needle down and back up the line a little further along. Pull the needle a little way through, but not completely. Wrap the working thread over the top and underneath the needle, and pull gently to form a loop.

2. Repeat step 1, a little to the side and down from the top of the first stitch (i.e. not through the bottom of the loop). Repeat as required.

Blanket (19)

1. Come up through the fabric. Using the sewing method push the needle through the fabric from bottom left to top right. The needle should come out level with where the thread first came up, and in front of the working thread.

2. Pull the needle through, catching the stitch on the working thread. Repeat. Secure with an anchor stitch in the final stitch.

Whipped running (20)

1. Stitch a straight line of running stitch.

2. Thread your needle with a contrasting colour thread. Bring it back up through the fabric at the end of the last stitch. On top of the fabric, thread the needle through the first stitch from right to left. Repeat with the other stitches, making sure that you pass under each running stitch from the same side each time. Push the needle back through the fabric on the last stitch to finish neatly.

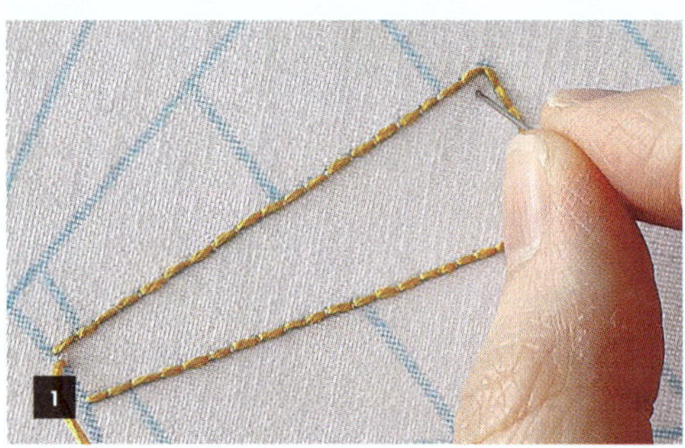

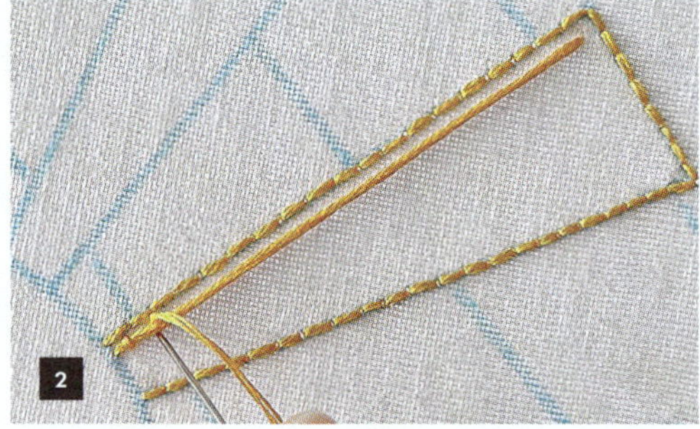

Couching (21)

1. Thread a needle with 6 strands of thread and tie a knot in one end. Stitch a large straight stitch and then leave the end loose for now. **2.** Thread a needle with 3 strands of thread. At the top end of the thread, come up through the fabric close to the couching thread. Stitch a small straight stitch over the top. Repeat at regular intervals, tying off both threads when complete.

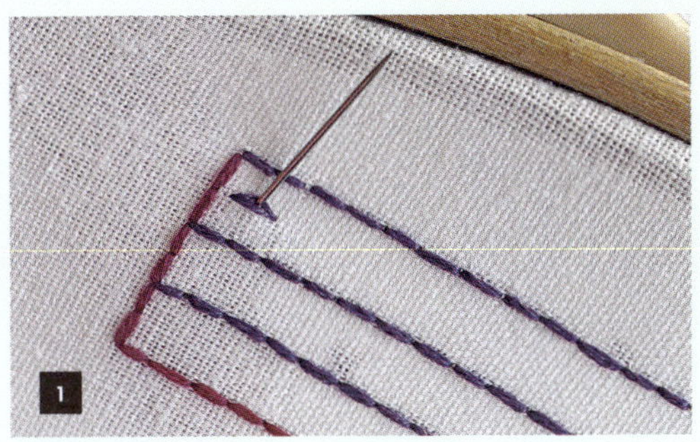

Split (22)

1. Come up through the fabric and make a single straight stitch at the desired length. Come back up through the middle of it, so that you are literally splitting the stitch.

2. Push the needle back through the fabric further along the line to be stitched, making a stitch that is the same size as the first one. Continue as required.

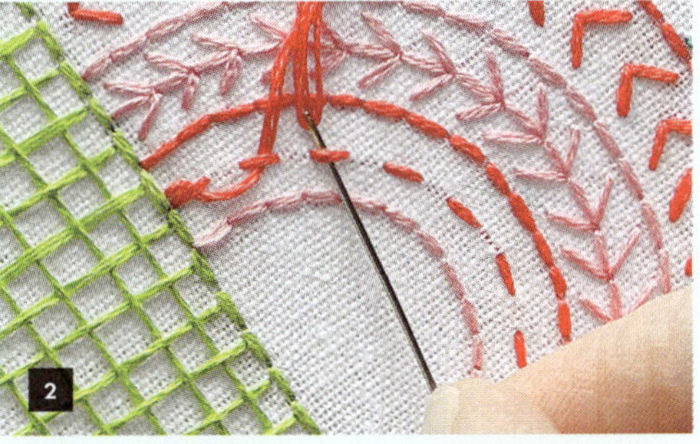

Laced running (23)

1. Stitch a wide running stitch along the line to be stitched. At the end of the line, come back up to the front. Thread it under the first stitch and then up through the next stitch along. Don't pull too tightly and leave a loop of thread between the stitches.

2. Come out over the top of the stitch and thread your needle through the top of the next stitch along, leaving another loop of thread between these stitches too. Repeat stitches as required.

Bosnian (24)

1. Stitch a single, vertical straight stitch, and repeat at regular intervals along the line to be stitched.

2. At the end of the line, come up at the bottom end of the final stitch. Push it back through at the top of the next stitch along to create a diagonal line between the two. Repeat until you reach the end of the line.

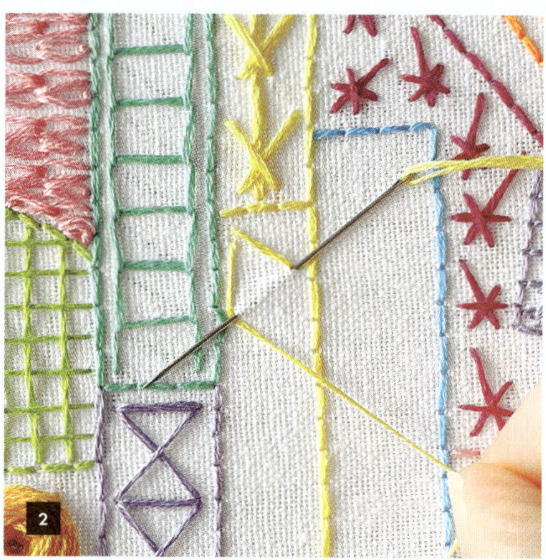

Closed buttonhole (25)

1. Come up through the fabric. Using the sewing method push the needle back through diagonally and back through to where the working thread comes out of the fabric. Pull the thread through to make a straight stitch.

2. Use the sewing method to push the needle through the opposite end of the straight stitch, and come up at a point which makes a triangle. Make sure the working thread goes under the needle. Gently pull the working thread so it catches on the needle to make the stitch. Repeat as required, adding the next diagonal straight stitch so it is adjacent to the first triangle.

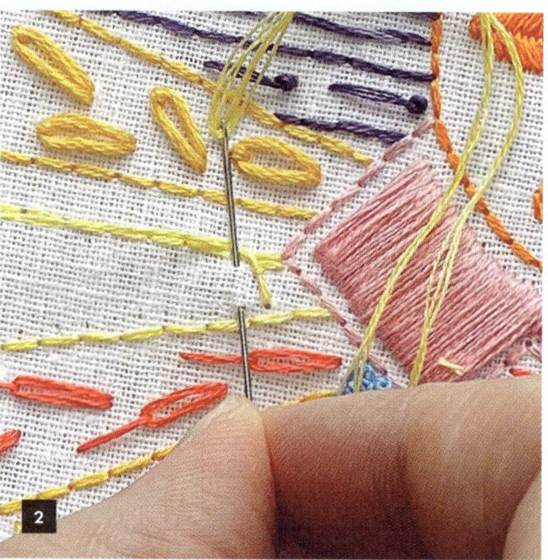

Buttonhole (26)

1. Bring your needle up through the fabric and, moving to the left, use the sewing method to create a vertical stitch downwards. Pull the needle through and catch the loop in the top left corner to create a small knot.

2. Move the working thread to the left and create the second stitch in the same way, using the sewing method and pulling up to the top left corner. Continue as required.

Chevron (27)

1. Stitch a small horizontal straight stitch. Come back up through the centre, without splitting it. Use the sewing method to add another horizontal stitch on the top of the line, diagonally to the right and working towards the left.

2. Bring the needle over the top and use the sewing method to stitch another straight stitch. This should be the same distance away from the one at the other side, and will come out at the same central point. Repeat these steps, alternating from the top to the bottom and creating a chevron effect.

Twisted chain (28)

1. Come up through the fabric just to the right of the end of the line to be stitched (draw a line on the fabric if it's helpful). Cross over the working thread and push it back through the fabric a little further down and diagonally to the left. Come up through the loop, down and in line with where you first came up through the fabric. Gently pull to tighten the twisted chain.

2. Move the needle over the working thread again and push it back through the fabric to the left and further down from where you came up. Come up through this second loop, down and in line with where you first came up through the fabric. Repeat as required, and use a small anchor stitch on the final stitch.

Petal (29)

1. Come up through the fabric at the right-hand end of the line to be stitched. Push it back further along to make a straight stitch around 1 cm long. Come up through the centre and to the side of this stitch, but don't split it. Push your needle back through the fabric right next to this, and leave a loop of your working thread.

2. Bring the needle back up at the end of the loop, and use the sewing method to take your needle further along the original straight line, as if it were right next to the original stitch. Create another straight stitch by pushing your needle back through the fabric at the base of the chain stitch. Continue stitching by starting another straight stitch directly next to the first one along the line.

Chained feather (30)

1. Come up through the fabric and push it back through right next to where you came up to make a slanted chain stitch. Come up through the loop and use the sewing method to start another chain stitch a little further down and slanted in the opposite direction.

2. Make a second slanted chain stitch, bringing your needle back up through the loop at the bottom of the long stem of the first chain stitch. Repeat as required, alternating the direction of the chain stitches.

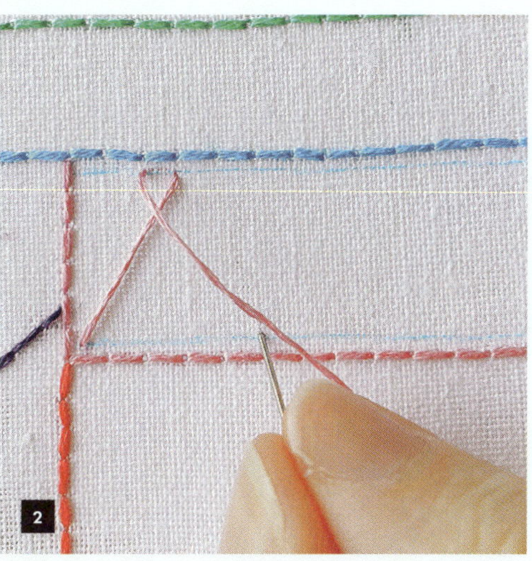

Herringbone (31)

1. Draw two parallel horizontal lines on the fabric with an erasable pen. Come up through the fabric at the left hand side of the bottom line, and push it through the top line diagonally to the right.

2. Come back up slightly to the left on the top line. Make another diagonal stitch to the right and push the needle back through the fabric on the bottom line. Come back up slightly to the left on the bottom line, and repeat both steps as required.

Zig zag chain (32)

1. Come up through the fabric. Use the sewing method to push the needle back through right next to this point, coming out diagonally a little further down. Wrap the working thread around the needle and gently pull it to catch the loop.

2. Use the sewing method push the needle back through right next to this point, coming out diagonally a little further down again in the opposite direction. Create chain stitches in a similar way as required, alternating direction each time. Secure the final stitch with a small anchor stitch.

photo banner

Make a special banner for any occasion by printing a photo onto fabric using t-shirt printing transfer paper. Add your choice of decorative trim for an extra flourish.

Stitches: cable, straight, twisted chain, scroll, laced running, Bosnian, Cretan, zig-zag chain, chevron, star.

You will need

- T-shirt printing transfer paper (I used the paper for lighter fabrics)
- A digital photo and a printer
- Two pieces of white cotton measuring 37 x 37cm (14½ x 14½" and 33 x 27cm (13 x 10"). This size is a guide so allow a generous allowance for your frame
- A plastic snap frame
- Thread - dark pink (601), light pink (604), medium tangerine (741), bright yellow (973), lime green (16), teal (3851), bright blue (3846) bright purple (3837)
- A fine tip water erasable pen
- A quilting ruler
- A handful of pins
- An iron
- A heat erasable pen
- A rotary cutter & cutting mat
- Sewing machine
- Gütermann sew-all thread in white (800) and bright teal (736)
- Roughly 18cm (7") length of giant pom pom trim in teal
- 30cm (12") cake dowel
- Length of thin macramé cord

We're really lucky where we live in Newcastle upon Tyne, in the north east of England, because we're close to the sea, the hills and the city. Although both of our children enjoy the beach, our daughter absolutely loves being by the sea and it's her happy place. The printed size of my photo is 15 x 19.5cm, but measurements are easy to adjust - use the size of your printed photo as a guide for the rest of the project. Don't be daunted by taking measurements - this project is a good place to start learning.

1

2

INSTRUCTIONS

1. Print out your photo in reverse onto the t-shirt transfer paper (following manufacturer's instructions and your printer instructions). Once dry, cut off any excess transfer paper around the image. Iron the fabric, before ironing the printed photo onto the fabric. If the instructions advise you to fix the image, make sure you do that too. Place the fabric in the clip frame.

2. Thread a needle with three strands of dark pink thread (601). Stitch a cable stitch around the straight edges of each side of the image. Make sure that your stitches are right next to the image without any gaps.

3. Remove the fabric from the snap frame. Use a quilting ruler and the fine tip water erasable pen to mark out the lines of the outer border. This border should be 1cm from the inside border you just stitched. Mark out the sections to be stitched, so there are three at the top and bottom, and four on the sides. Add squares in each corner.

4. Position the fabric back in the frame, and use the dark pink thread (601) and cable stitch to outline the outer border. Using 3 strands of the same thread, add small straight stitches to mark out each of the sections within the border.

5. Add the decorative stitches within each section, using 3 strands, starting from the top left corner moving around clockwise. Stitch the pattern twice as follows:

Twisted chain - light pink (604)
Scroll - medium tangerine (741)
Laced running - bright yellow (973)
Bosnian - lime green (16)
Cretan - teal (3851)
Zig zag chain - bright blue (3846)
Chevron - bright purple (3837)

When these stitches are complete, add small star stitches in each corner using 3 strands of dark pink thread (601).

6. Remove the fabric from the snap frame and iron around the edges. Use the quilting ruler and heat erasable pen to draw lines to mark out the outer edges

7

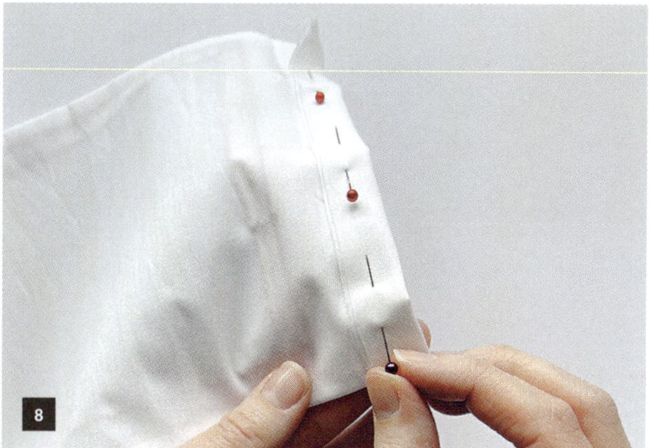
8

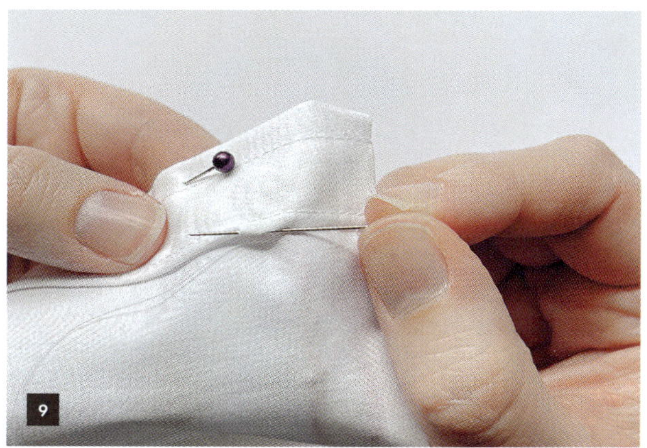
9

of the banner. These should be just over 1cm. You need to draw them on the sides and bottom edge (not the top for now). Take the second piece of white fabric and lay the stitched piece on top, right sides together. Pin together to secure.

7. Stitch along the border lines on your sewing machine, leaving the top of the banner open. Trim the seam allowance with a rotary cutter and carefully clip the corners of the seam allowance diagonally. Turn the right way out and press the border with a cool iron.

8. To make the top edge, fold over the excess fabric at the top to create a 1cm border that matches the sides and bottom edge. Press. Create another fold with about 1.5cm or so of fabric, trimming any excess with the rotary cutter. Pin this fold together (leaving the first border fold for now) to join the open edge. With your sewing machine, stitch two horizontal lines across the fold to join the open edges. Leave enough space between the two so that the dowel fits through (you might want to test this before you stitch!).

9. Fold the second fold over and use a slip stitch to join the two edges together (scan the QR code on page 118 for a video tutorial). Make sure that you don't stitch through the front of the banner. Cut a piece of pom pom trim to size, and then pin it onto the back piece of the banner. Use a slip stitch again to attach the trim to the reverse panel only with a matching thread colour. Cut the dowel to size and tie on the macramé cord. It's ready to display!

Stuff

couched rope basket

Couching is a wonderful stitch, and you don't just have to use embroidery thread to stitch it. Experiment with couching using Nova Vita yarn in this fun project.

Stitches: straight, couching.

You will need

- A small cotton rope basket (this is 15 x 13cm; approx 6 x 5")
- A seam ripper
- Nova Vita 12 recycled cotton yarn in shade 043
- Thread - dark sea green (958), cornflower (3838), light apricot (3824), lilac (209), light pink (604), dark pink (601 - this dark pink matches the Nova Vita yarn)
- A few pearl head pins
- Jewellery pliers (optional but extremely useful)

As well as patterns and colours, textures are something I've started to play around with more in my embroidery designs over the last couple of years. In this project I'm using DMC Nova Vita recycled cotton yarn, which is much thicker than stranded cotton but gives a wonderful 3D effect. Read the instructions below carefully before you start, as you'll need to take extra care with the pins so that you don't hurt yourself. If you don't have yarn like this, a nice thick woolly yarn would work just as well.

INSTRUCTIONS

1. Carefully remove any labels from your basket using a seam ripper. Thread a needle with 6 strands of cornflower thread (3838). Choose a place to start and come up from inside the basket to the front between two ropes. Push the needle back through to the inside to create a single stitch over the rope.

2

3

4

5

2. Repeat with the same colour, leaving gaps between the stitches. This will create a sort of speckled or sprinkle effect, so you can stitch as many or as few as you like.

3. When you have stitched all the way around the basket in this colour, repeat with the next colour. Leave gaps between each of the colours so that the basket is visible. Continue to do this with the remaining colours except the dark pink (601), until you are happy with the coverage.

4. Measure the Nova Vita yarn for each letter and cut it to the desired length. The easiest way to do this is to position the shape of each letter on the basket and cut to size. Always cut on the generous side rather than cutting too small - you can always trim it later if needed.

5. Carefully pin the pieces in position, except for the lines crossing the 't' and 'f's as these will be added later. I found that the easiest way to do this was to push the pins in vertically, so a small part of the pin goes through to the inside of the basket.

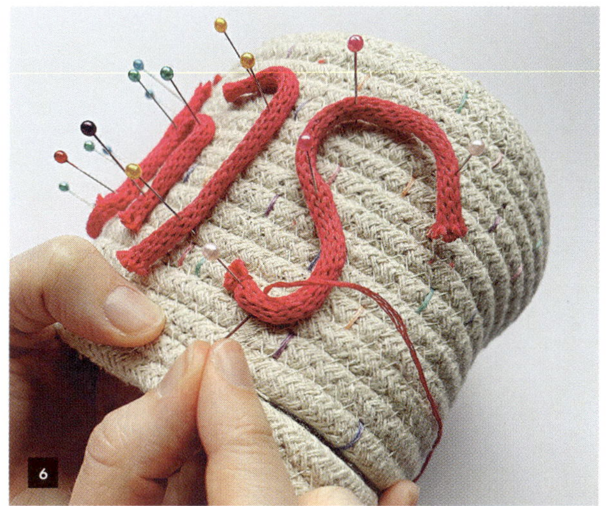

6. Use a couching stitch to attach the yarn to the basket. Make sure that you are extremely careful not to hurt your hands on the pins on the inside. You can use the jewellery pliers to help you pull the needle through to the inside of the basket. This should help you avoid any injuries. When you get to the end of the letter, don't tie it off but leave the thread loose.

7. When all of the pins have been removed, tie off the ends of the thread on the inside of the basket. Then pin the lines of the 't' and 'f's in position, trimming the yarn to size if they're a little bit long.

8. Stitch these final pieces in place, tying off at the back once the pins have been removed, as before. At this point, you can always add any additional colourful stitches on the basket if you feel it needs any. If you don't like the thread that's visible inside the basket, you could always line your basket with some coordinating fabric. I decided not to as I like the effect, but do whatever works for you.

JUST
ONE
MORE
PAGE

shelfie bookmark

It may be small, but this shelfie bookmark uses a lot of stitches! It's also a great way to experiment with using watercolour pencils on fabric if you've never tried it before.

Stitches: backstitch, split, satin, whipped backstitch, Bosnian, fly, Cretan, twisted chain, blanket, whipped running, straight, French knots.

You will need

- A 32 x 32cm (12½ x 12½") piece of white fabric
- 22cm (9") embroidery hoop to stitch in
- A fine tip water erasable pen
- Derwent Inktense watercolour pencils (I have the basic box of 12)
- A paintbrush and water
- An iron
- A heat erasable pen
- Thread - mid delft blue (799), light red (3705), mid apricot (3340), ocean blue (824), light green (164), mid forest green (988), dark sea green (958), magenta (917), mid beige (739), yellow (726), mid yellow (725), brown (3826), black (310) white (blanc)
- An iron
- 19.5 x 4.5cm (approx 8 x 2") piece of white Plasticard
- Some Scotch tape
- 20 x 5cm (8 x 2") piece of wool or acrylic white felt
- Rotary cutter and cutting mat

This sweet shelfie bookmark is a perfect project to use every day, and it's much nicer than using a random piece of paper as a bookmark. The little cat is a reference to my lovely friend Daria who lived in Japan for a while, where the maneki-neko or beckoning cat brings good luck. Whenever I see a waving cat, I always think of her. I'd recommend doing a test swatch of the pencil colours on a scrap of fabric before you start, so that you can see how much the colours change and run on the fabric once you've added water.

1

2

INSTRUCTIONS

1. Use the fine tip water erasable pen to draw the outer edges of the books, shelves, plant pot and leaves, lucky cat and vase onto the fabric. Use the Inktense watercolour pencils to shade in the elements. Then use a paintbrush to wash over the colours to make them more vibrant, fixing the colours with a cool iron as you go.

2. Trace the rest of the design with a heat erasable pen and place the fabric in the hoop for stitching. Using 3 strands of colours matching each element of the design, stitch small backstitches around the edges of the books and vase.

3. Stitch the plant by adding small split stitches along the lines of the plant pot, using 3 strands of mid beige thread (739). Then add the plant details with small backstitches using light green (164) for the stems and mid forest green (988) for the leaves. Add the foliage in the vase at the bottom with 3 strands of mid beige thread (739), stitching straight stitches with French knots at the top.

4. The lucky cat is stitched with a whipped backstitch around the edges, using 3 strands of yellow thread (726). Add the collar using small satin stitches, using 3 strands of light red thread (3705) around the neck, and 3 strands of mid yellow (725) for the medal. Add the facial features using 1 strand of black (310) in small backstitches.

5. Add a variety of decorative stitches to the spines of the books. The colours and stitches are as follows (using 3 strands throughout):
Top shelf: straight, mid delft blue (799)
Second shelf: fly, ocean blue (824); Bosnian, light green (164)
Third shelf: Cretan, dark sea green (958); twisted chain, magenta (917)
Bottom shelf: blanket, mid apricot (3340); whipped

6a

7a

8

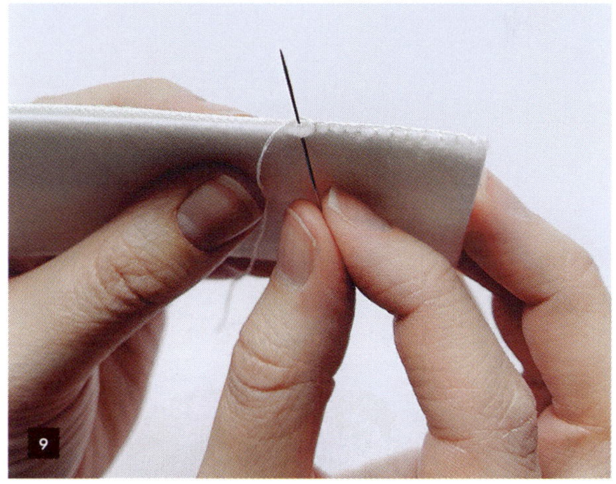
9

running, yellow (726) and mid apricot (3340)

6. Stitch around the shelves with a fairly long backstitch, using 3 strands of brown (3826). Add the text using 2 strands of black (310), and stitch small backstitches in the direction of the text.

7. When complete, remove the fabric from the hoop and iron around the stitching. Use a heat erasable pen to draw a border round the stitching, roughly 1-1.5cm away from the edge. Carefully cut along these lines around the stitching and discard the excess fabric.

8. Place the stitching face down on a flat surface. Take the Plasticard and position it over the top so all the stitching is covered, and fold the excess fabric over the Plasticard. Secure it in place on the back with some Scotch tape. Measure and cut a piece of white felt to the same size as your bookmark. Cut it out with a rotary cutter for a really neat edge.

9. Use a really small blanket stitch to attach the front to the back piece of felt, using 2 strands of white thread. Try not to take the stitching through the front, but use the folded edge at the sides to join it to the back to make it look really neat. Your bookmark is complete.

simple stitched place mats

If you want to begin to customise homewares then place mats are a great place to start. They're so easy to stitch on, and come ready-made in a wide variety of colours.

Stitches: buttonhole, split, Cretan, whipped backstitch, closed buttonhole, cable, chained feather.

You will need

- A set of place mats (depending on how many places you can fit at your table)
- A seam ripper
- An iron
- A water erasable pen and brush pen
- Thread - navy 311, mid turquoise (3810), dark turquoise (3808)
- Perle no. 8 in white (blanc) and very light sky blue (747)
- A long quilting ruler (or similar long ruler)

Homewares are brilliant for stitching on, and it's really fun to add your own customised stitching to mass-produced items to make them bespoke to you. You can easily match colours to your home, and this is a great, simple project that you can pick up and put down as often as you like. It's up to you how much customisation you add to these place mats. I decided to only stitch down one side, as I liked the look of it as I was stitching the project. It's okay to change and adapt your plan as you work on a project.

1

2

INSTRUCTIONS

1. Carefully remove any labels with a seam ripper, and iron the place mats. Place on a flat surface and put a dinner plate on top, so that you can measure the stitch-able space on each short edge. Mark with the water erasable pen.

2. Using a long ruler, draw a series of lines to mark out the design on one side. These can be drawn in any way you like, so play around with the spacing until you're happy, Refer to the rough guide in the templates section to copy my design. Leave larger gaps for the bigger stitches as shown.

3

4

5

6

3. Stitch the third line from the right with split stitch. Use 3 strands of navy thread (311) making sure the stitches start and end right at the top and bottom edges.

4. Between the two lines to the right of the split stitch, add a line of buttonhole stitch. Start the stitches on the line adjacent to the split stitch with the 'spokes' pointing to the centre of the mat. Use 3 strands of mid turquoise thread (3810).

5. Now working towards the left, add a line of Cretan stitch using white (blanc) Perle thread. I stitched this freestyle, but you can always use your water erasable pen to mark out where the tops and bottoms of the stitches should be if you prefer.

6. To the left of the Cretan stitch, add a line of whipped backstitch using 3 strands of dark turquoise thread (3808).

7

8

9

7. The next stitch along is a line of closed buttonhole stitch, which is stitched using very light sky blue Perle (747). Again, I stitched this freestyle but you can draw on the triangles first if you prefer. Add a line of cable stitch next to this in dark turquoise (3808).

8. The final section to add on the end of the design is a row of chained feather, which is stitched using white (blanc) Perle thread. I turned the place mat around to stitch this because it was easier to handle the fabric, but if you want the leaves to point upwards then just stitch as before.

9. Once all the stitching is complete, remove the visible pen lines with your brush pen - or you could just give the place mats a gentle wash and an iron if you prefer.

The way you talk to yourself matters.

sort-of mandala hoop

Lots of the stitches in this chapter work really well in circular designs. This project is designed to showcase some of my favourite border and edging stitches.

Stitches: split, blanket, petal, herringbone, backstitch, rope, coral, laced running.

You will need

- 32 x 32cm (12½ x 12½") light cream or off-white cotton fabric
- A fine tip water erasable pen
- 18cm (7") embroidery hoop to display the stitching
- 20cm (8") embroidery hoop for stitching in (optional)
- Thread - dark antique blue (3750), mid antique blue (931), very light sky blue (747), bright sea green (959), quartz pink (3713), light coral (352), pale pumpkin (3825)
- Perle no.8 thread in bright sea green (959)

Mandala means 'circle' in Sanskrit and is a geometric pattern often used as an aid to meditation. Mandalas usually contain a variety of shapes to create the pattern, but I wanted to use the stitches within circles to form the patterns (which is why it's called a 'sort-of' mandala). This circular design reminds me of rings inside a tree, with the words flowing through the middle to give it strength. The colour palette is more natural than my usual rainbow style, but I really enjoyed getting out of my comfort zone and finding new inspiration.

1

INSTRUCTIONS

1. Carefully trace the design onto the fabric, ignoring the outer line which indicates the hoop size. Place the fabric in your larger hoop. Stitch the second largest circle using 3 strands of mid antique blue thread (931) and small split stitches. I'm using the reverse technique here, where instead of coming up through the middle of the stitch, you stitch more like backstitch and go down through the middle instead. Miss out a circle moving inwards, and stitch the next one in using the same stitch in quartz pink thread (3713).

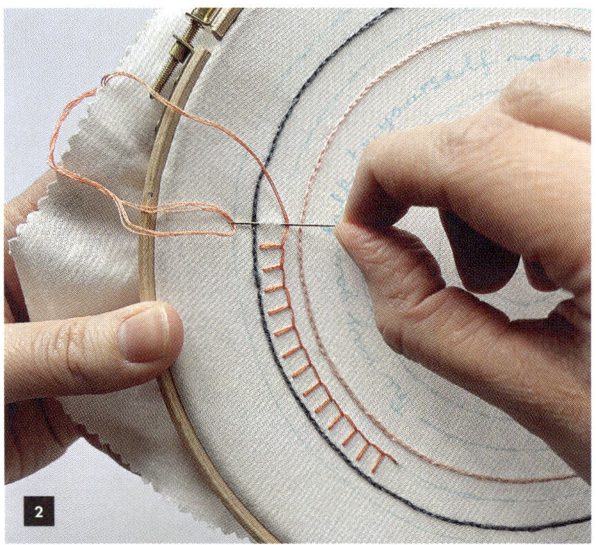

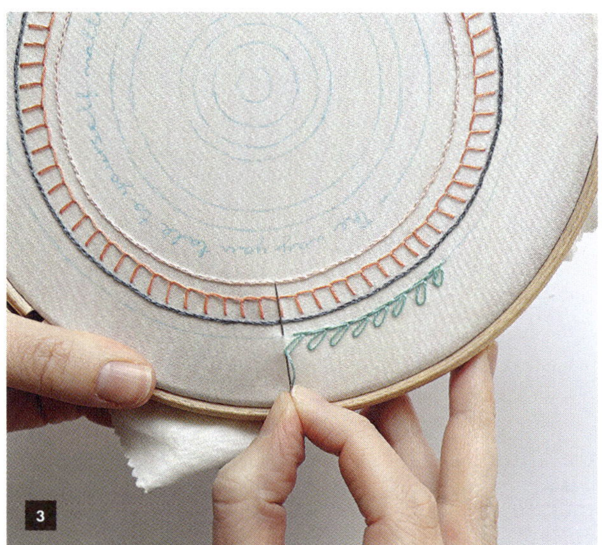

2. In between the two split stitch circles, add a circle of blanket stitch using 3 strands of light coral thread (352). The 'spokes' of the blanket stitch should point towards the outer edge of the hoop as shown.

3. On the outer circle, stitch a small petal stitch using the teal Perle thread. You need to keep the petals fairly small, as they need to fit into the 18cm hoop once stitching is complete.

4. Stitch the circle below the text using split stitch, with 3 strands of pale pumpkin thread (3825). Then add herringbone stitches between the next two smaller circles using 3 strands of quartz pink thread (3713).

5. After this, the next circle towards the centre is created with coral stitch. Use 3 strands of mid antique blue thread (931), and keep the knots as evenly spaced around the circle as possible.

6

7

8

9

6. In the central circle, stitch a running stitch in the same mid antique blue thread (931) and then add the laced running stitch with three strands of the light coral (352).

7. Stitch the semicircle with 3 strands of dark antique blue thread (3750), using rope stitch. Keep the stitches evenly spaced to ensure a similar thickness and texture along the line.

8. Add the text with small backstitches, using 2 strands of the dark antique blue thread (3750). Remember to stitch in the direction of the text as if you were writing it by hand.

9. When complete, remove any visible pen lines with the brush pen. Position in a painted hoop that tones with the colours as I have done. Finish the back ready to display your work.

chapter 4: decorative stitches & motifs

In this chapter, we're going to be stitching some of the stitches that are standalone motifs, patterns or decorations in themselves. You can get really creative with how you use them, whether that's filling in areas with stitches, using them to create patterns or just individually as stitches within a design. Some of the projects in this chapter have a bit more scope to change the stitches. So if a design includes a stitch that you're not sure about or you would simply prefer to use a different one, then just get creative and change it!

Woven cross (33)

1. Stitch a cross stitch, starting from bottom left to top right and then top left to bottom right. Come back up in the bottom left corner, and then stitch another stitch up to the top right corner. Use the sewing method to come back up in the bottom right corner.

2. Thread the needle through the two diagonal stitches in the bottom left, going under the first and over the second. Push your needle back down through the fabric in the top left corner, and tie off at the back.

Long-tail daisy (34)

1. Stitch a small chain stitch, coming up through the bottom of the loop

2. Add a longer straight stitch to the bottom to secure the stitch.

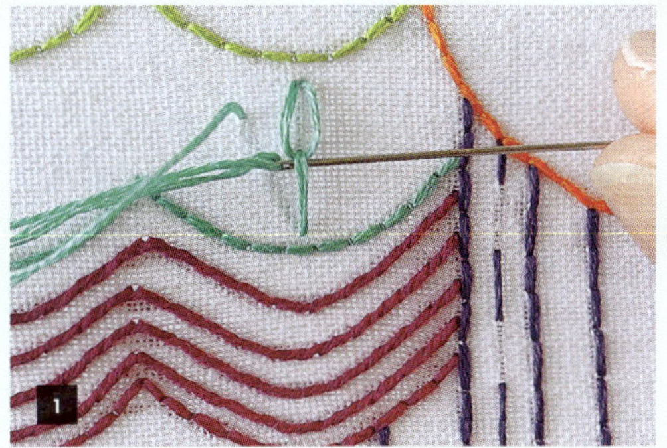

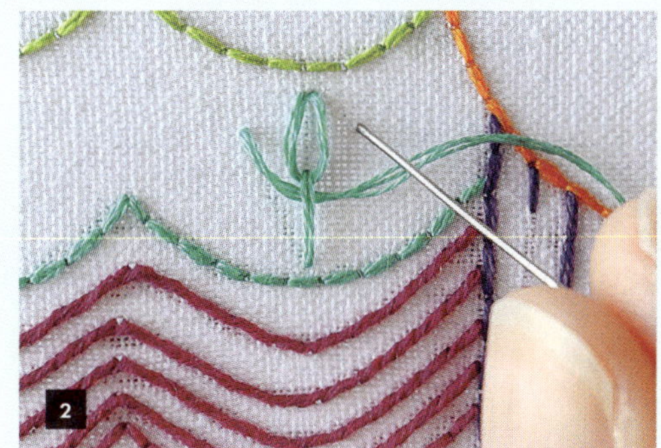

Tulip (35)

1. Stitch a long-tail daisy, tying off at the back for neatness if you prefer.

2. Come back up through the fabric, to the left and centre of the loop. Thread the needle underneath the straight stitch without going through the fabric. Push your needle back through the fabric to the right and centre of the loop. Gently tie off at the back.

Brick and cross (36)

1. Stitch a simple cross stitch. To one side, stitch three evenly spaced, horizontal straight stitches. The middle one should line up with the centre of the cross.

2. Repeat alternately, both horizontally and vertically, to create a pattern.

Arrowhead (37)

1. Stitch a small diagonal straight stitch from bottom right to the top point. Repeat on the other side, working towards the point.

2. Repeat as required, either in a line to create a pattern or more randomly to fill a space.

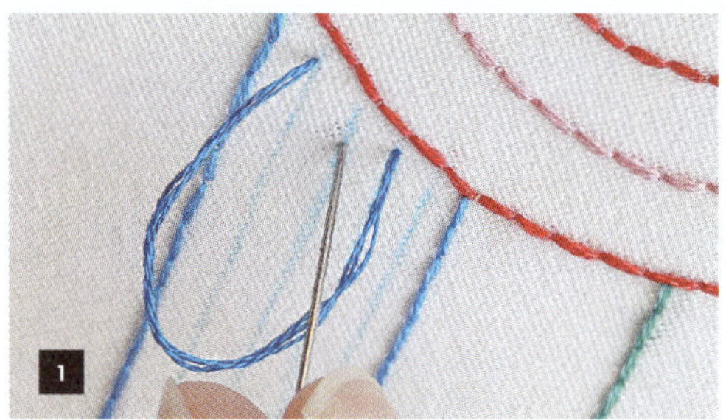

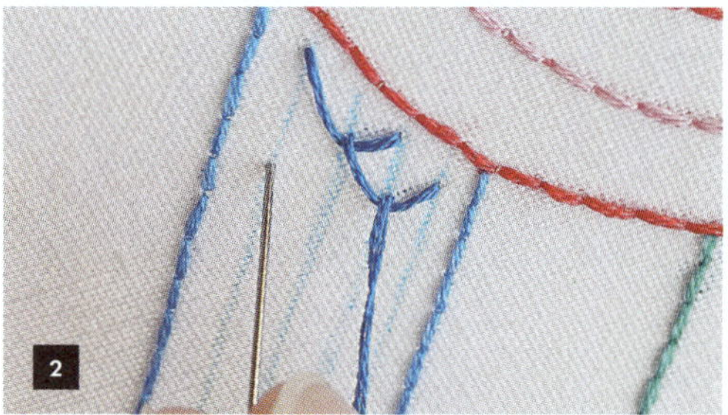

Feather (38)

1. Draw four evenly spaced, vertical lines on the fabric with an erasable pen. The lines L-R are numbered 1-4. Come up at the end of 1 and push it through at the end of 3. Come up a little further down at 2 and pull gently to catch the loop.

2. Push the needle through the fabric on line 4, slightly lower but almost level with where you came up on line 2. Gently pull the thread to catch the loop. Repeat as required, adding a small anchor stitch on the final loop to secure it in place.

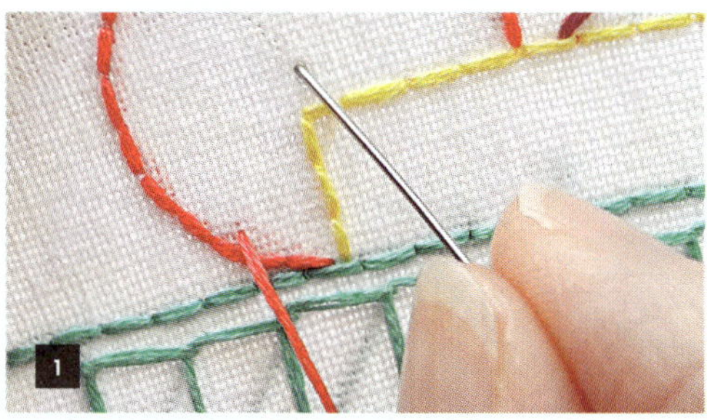

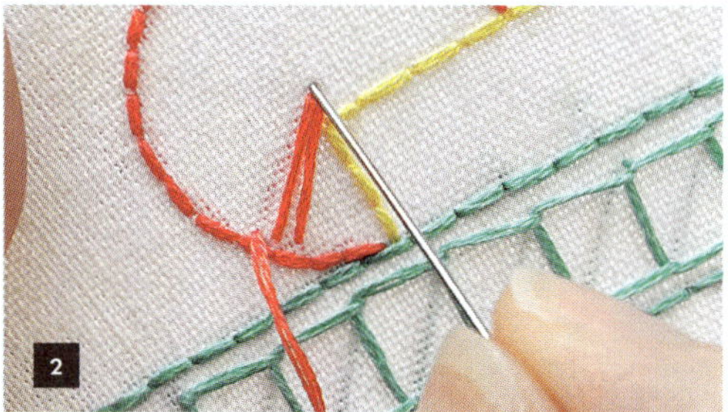

Eyelet (39)

1. Using a blunt tapestry needle, make a hole in the centre of the circle where the eyelet is to be stitched. Working from the outer edge, stitch a straight stitch towards the centre. Push the needle through the hole.

2. Stitch more straight stitches, leaving similarly sized gaps between each one, working towards the centre. Repeat until the whole circle is complete.

Pistil (40)

1. Come up through the fabric at the opposite end to where you want the Pistil knot to be. Wrap the thread around your needle three times. Push the needle into the fabric where the knot will be positioned.

2. Gently pull the thread to the bottom of the needle, and then pull through to create the knot. Tie off gently at the back.

Thorn (41)

1. Using 6 strands of thread, stitch a single straight stitch to be couched. Thread another needle with 6 strands of the same colour. Bring it up through the fabric at one end, slightly further down and out a little. Stitch a cross stitch over the top.

2. Keep stitching cross stitches over the couched thread, making the crosses bigger as you move along and slightly more top-heavy as they get bigger. Tie off both threads at the bottom.

Sheaf (42)

1. Stitch a vertical straight stitch, roughly 1 cm in length. Stitch two more either side. Come up through the fabric, so you come out in the centre next to the left hand stitch.

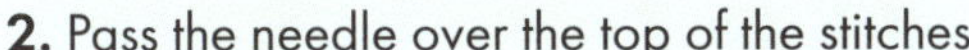

2. Pass the needle over the top of the stitches and then pass it underneath, without going through the fabric. Repeat once more and pull the working thread gently, to gather the straight stitches together in the middle. Push your needle back down through the fabric in the centre and tie off at the back.

Scallop (43)

1. Come up through the fabric, and push it through at the point where it creates the desired stitch width. Come back up at the bottom of the scallop.

2. Gently pull the thread to catch the loop. Secure in place with a small anchor stitch.

Leaf (44)

1. Draw a leaf shape onto the fabric with an erasable pen. Stitch a small vertical straight stitch from the top point of the leaf. Add a diagonal stitch just below it, going back through the fabric below the first stitch. Repeat on the other side.

2. Repeat, alternating sides and moving down the leaf shape to cover it. Follow the outline of the leaf as you stitch.

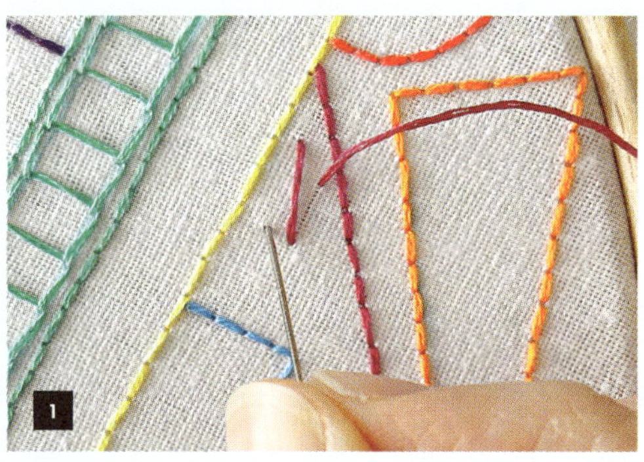

Ermine (45)

1. Stitch a vertical straight stitch. A little way down from the top and to the right, come back up and cross over to the left. Push the needle through the fabric a little way up from the bottom of the vertical stitch.

2. Repeat on the other side, creating a mirror image of the diagonal stitch.

Double fern (46)

1. Stitch a small vertical straight stitch, from top to bottom. To the right and slightly down, add another and make sure that it joins the first stitch exactly where it ended. Repeat on the other side.

2. Repeat working outwards, adding one more diagonal stitch on each side.

Buttonhole wheel (47)

1. Use an erasable pen to draw a circle made up of 7 dots, with one in the centre. Come up through the central dot, and push it back through one outer dot. Leave a loop of thread free and come back up at the next dot, catching the thread.

2. Hold the working thread and push your needle through the central dot. Catch the loop when you bring the needle back up through the fabric at the next dot along. Repeat around the circle, and secure the last stitch with an anchor stitch.

Whipped wheel (48)

1. Draw a five-spoked wheel onto the fabric. Stitch each spoke with a straight stitch from the outer edge towards the centre. Come up through the fabric as close as you can to the centre. Weave the needle under the closest spoke.

2. Move the needle back over and under the same spoke, as well as the next one. Make sure the thread moves close to the centre of the wheel. Repeat, moving back over one and under two spokes each time, until the whole wheel is covered. Remove any visible pen lines when complete.

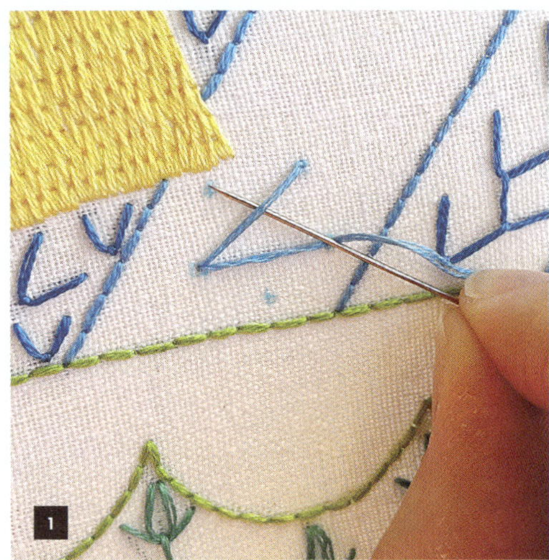

Woven star (49)

1. Draw 5 dots in a circle on your fabric with an erasable pen. Number the dots 1-5 from the top working clockwise. Come up at 1 and take it down at 4 to make a straight stitch. Bring it up at 2 and go back in the same point at 4, and then come back up at 2, and slide the needle under the first stitch. Push the needle back through the fabric at 5.

2. Come up at 3. Slide your needle over the first stitch and under the second, before pushing the needle back through at 5. Come back up at 3, and slide your needle over the first stitch and under the second, before pushing the needle back through at 1. Tie off at the back.

Open chain (50)

1. Draw two parallel horizontal lines with an erasable pen. Come up through the fabric on the right end of the bottom line. Use the sewing method and insert your needle at the right side of the top line, coming out diagonally left on the bottom line with the working thread behind.

2. Pull the working thread a little to create a loop, and then insert the needle at the top of this loop, coming out diagonally left again as before. Repeat, making a longer chain of loops, and secure the final one in place with an anchor stitch in each corner.

Closed feather (51)

1. Come up through the fabric, and push it down to the right about 1cm away. Leave a loop and come back up a little way down from where you started the first stitch to catch it. Push your needle back through the fabric on the other side of the first stitch, going through the fabric at the same point.

2. Leave a loop, and come back up the fabric at a point that makes a triangle as shown. Repeat as required.

Zig zag (52)

1. Come up through the fabric and make a vertical straight stitch. Come back up where you started and stitch a diagonal straight stitch towards the bottom left. Come up through the fabric at the top and add another vertical stitch to meet the end of the diagonal stitch. Repeat along the line.

2. Add an additional vertical straight stitch over the one at the end. Then come back up at the top again to create a diagonal stitch to the right. Add another vertical stitch here and repeat to the other end of the line.

DMC 307

patchwork needlebook

A needlebook is a really handy project to make, and the inside pockets for scissors and bobbins are perfect for taking your stitching with you anywhere.

Stitches: zig zag, woven star, open chain, ermine, brick and cross, woven cross, closed feather, running.

You will need

- 7 strips of different plain coloured fabrics, measuring 24 x 3cm (9 x 1″) each
- Thread - light purple (340), light pink (604), light apricot (3824), primrose (727), pale lime (15), bright sea green (959), baby blue (3755)
- Hand-dyed silk embroidery thread (or variegated if you can source it more easily)
- A 23 x 15cm (9 x 6″) piece of lining fabric
- A 23 x 15cm (9 x 6″) and two 19 x 12cm (7 x 5″) pieces of white felt
- Two pieces measuring 15 x 10cm (6 x 4″) and 12 x 10cm (5 x 4″) of glitter vinyl fabric
- Some pins
- A sewing machine (optional)
- An iron
- A fine tip water erasable pen
- A ruler
- Gütermann thread, shade 1 or 800
- Some quilting clips (optional)
- Rico 2cm cotton bias binding in neon pink
- A sew-in label (optional)

Patchwork is fun, but I'm not that good at measuring accurately! Smaller projects are great, because you can practise techniques on a small scale and build up your confidence. I used my sewing machine to put this together, but it would be a wonderful project to sew by hand too. The glitter vinyl is amazing to sew with, and I'm sure that I'll be using it more in future. I've also used some beautiful hand-dyed thread made by my friend Tracey (What Mustard Made) to stitch the spine, and it's just gorgeous to work with.

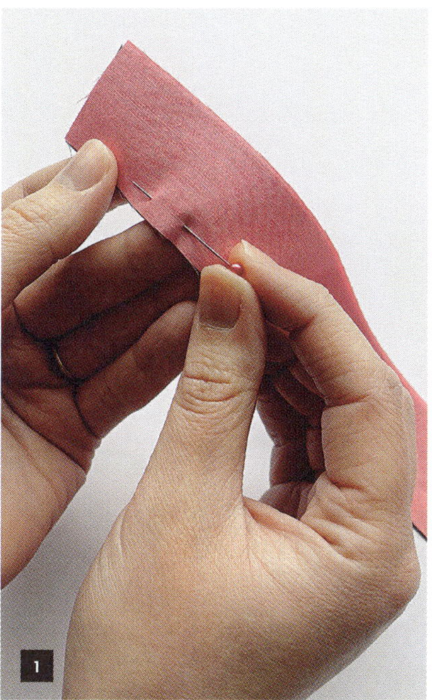
1

2

INSTRUCTIONS

1. Carefully cut out the strips of fabric and lay them on a flat surface. Work out the order of the colours as you'd like them to appear on the finished project. Take the top two strips of fabric and position them right sides together. Pin in place and then stitch along the edge with a 0.5cm seam allowance.

2. Repeat with the remaining strips of fabric. When they are all complete, press the seams towards the top.

3

4

5

6

3. Place the patchwork face up on top of the piece of white felt. Pin it into place. Use a ruler and a fine tip water erasable pen to mark on the central lines that will form the spine of the needlebook - you can use the template in the final chapter as a guide.

4. Add the decorative stitches to secure the patchwork to the felt layer. I matched the thread to the fabric colour, but you can mix this up if you want to. The colours and stitches from top to bottom are as follows:
Light purple (340) - zig zag
Light pink (604) - woven star
Light apricot (3824) - open chain
Primrose (727) - ermine
Pale lime (15) - brick and cross
Bright sea green (959) - woven cross
Baby blue (3755) - closed feather

Once the decorative stitching is complete, trim the short sides of the patchwork so it is the same size as the felt. Don't trim the top or the bottom of the felt as it will be used to attach the bias binding later.

5. Measure a piece of bias binding so it fits down one long edge and the top edge of the smaller piece of glitter vinyl fabric. Cut to size, and then pin in place. Attach using your sewing machine (I did this in one go by making sure the binding overlapped in the right place, but take your time with this and stitch each side separately if it's new to you). Repeat with the long edge of the bigger piece.

6. Pin the larger piece of the glitter vinyl to the left side of the lining fabric. Make sure the pins are close to the edge, or you'll puncture the vinyl with the pins and it will be visible when finished. Sew it in place on your sewing machine, with a small seam allowance of 3-4mm. Repeat with the smaller piece, positioning it in the bottom right corner. Use a small slip stitch and the same thread from your sewing machine to secure the bound edge of the smaller pocket to the lining.

7. Place the lining fabric and the patchwork wrong sides together, and use some quilting clips to secure it in position. If you don't have any quilting pins, sewing pins will work just fine. Stitch roughly 3mm all the way around the outer edge on your machine to attach everything together.

8. Place the needlebook on a flat surface, with the inside facing upwards. Take the two 19 x 12cm pieces of white felt and line them up in the centre. Pin in place to secure, and then stitch along the centre on your sewing machine. Thread your needle with a length of the hand-dyed thread. The spine will be secured with 3 lines of running stitch, and it's helpful to start with the central one first because you can follow the line of the machine stitching. Stitch one row of running stitch along this line, then turn the needlebook around and stitch another one in the gaps as shown.

9. Pin and/or clip the bias binding around the edge of the needlebook. Stitch along the edges on your machine to secure it in place. For an extra touch, add a little label above the scissor pocket with slip stitch.

TEAMWORK
makes the
DREAM WORK

stitched framed print

A hand stitched print is a really simple project, but it's so effective. Choose a lighter background fabric colour if you're not confident stitching on a dark fabric.

Stitches: whipped backstitch, arrowhead, scallop, double fern, long-tail daisy, sheaf, pistil, ermine, tulip, split (or reverse split), backstitch.

You will need

- 23 x 40cm (9 x 16") piece of dark blue fabric
- White Aqua Trick pen and brush pen
- Thread - white (blanc), red (349), mid apricot (3340), bright yellow (973), nile green (954), dark sea green (958), bright blue (3846), light purple (340), light rose pink (3716), plus Light Effects gold (E3821)
- A 22 x 30cm (9 x 12") tapestry frame or clip frame to stitch in
- An iron
- Rotary cutter and ruler
- A rectangular picture frame to display your stitching in

I tend to display most of my work in painted embroidery hoops, but it's nice to have alternative ways to showcase your projects. You can pick up relatively cheap frames in a variety of shapes and sizes on the high street, or look in vintage or charity shops for more unique finds. This phrase is something we say to our children, and I thought it would be lovely to stitch as a reminder. I'm often asked how to transfer designs onto dark fabrics, so I've used my favourite method of doing this here - a white Prym Aqua Trick marker.

1

INSTRUCTIONS

1. Trace the design onto your fabric. If you're using a dark fabric like this one then you might find it easier to use a light box to help (or stick it to a window with washi tape). You don't need to trace all of the decorative markings within the lettering if you don't want to - just draw on whatever you need.

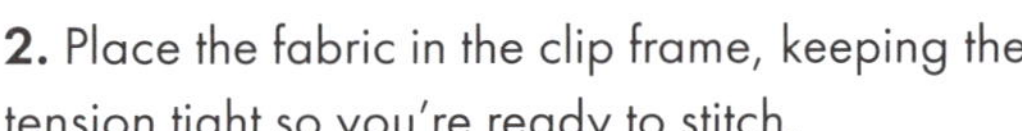

2. Place the fabric in the clip frame, keeping the tension tight so you're ready to stitch.

3. Thread your needle with three strands of white thread. Stitch small backstitches around the letter 't' in the word 'teamwork'. Whip the backstitches around the letter, and then repeat with the rest of the letters in the same word. The words 'dream' and 'work' are also stitches using whipped backstitch, and should be stitched in white thread too.

4. Add the decorative stitches within the word 'teamwork' using three strands of thread for each colour. I have used them in rainbow order here, but feel free to mix it up however you like. The colours and stitches are as follows:

T - red (349), arrowhead
E - mid apricot (3340), scallop
A - bright yellow (973), double fern
M - nile green (954), long-tail daisy
W - dark sea green (958), sheaf
O - bright blue (3846), pistil
R - light purple (340), ermine
K - light rose pink (3716), tulip

5. Use split stitch to stitch the centres of the words

'dream' and 'work' using three strands of light effects gold (E3821). Here I'm using what's commonly known as reverse split stitch, where instead of coming up through the middle of each stitch, you work it more like a backstitch but split each stitch when you go back down through the fabric.

6. Stitch the words 'makes the' using small backstitches. I used 3 strands of white thread but you could change the colour if you prefer. You could also whip this section too for a smooth finish.

7. Remove any visible pen with a brush pen. Take your time as it can take longer to remove if it has been on the fabric a while.

8. Take the finished stitching out of the clip frame, and iron around the edges. Place it on a flat surface, face down. Take the back out of the frame, and lay it on top to work out the positioning. Trim down any excess fabric with a rotary cutter, making sure that you do this a little at a time because you can't put it back if you've trimmed it too much!

9. Position the stitching in the frame, and secure the back so that it's ready to display.

BSERVER'S BOO
OF
WILD FLOWERS
THE O

botanical hoop

Botanicals are popular in embroidery, and it's easy to see why! This small hoop uses lots of decorative stitches to create a colourful design inspired by nature.

Stitches: leaf, straight, satin, backstitch, thorn, chained feather, eyelet, whipped wheel, French knots.

You will need

- A 15cm (6") embroidery hoop
- 22 x 22cm (9 x 9") yellow fabric
- Thread - light teal (964), mid deep water green (992), deep water green (3814), dark deep water green (991), sand gold (677), pale cream (746)
- A heat erasable pen to transfer the design
- A tapestry needle for eyelet stitch

Nature is so inspiring, and this project brings a modern twist to botanicals with the use of bright yellow fabric and shades of teal thread. This design is a little different from my usual style, but I loved experimenting with creating the natural elements for this hoop. Plants on pink have been a trend for quite some time, but maybe we should make leaves on yellow a thing too? You could stitch this design on any plain colour fabric, so raid your fabric stash and see what colour works best for you.

INSTRUCTIONS

1. Use the heat erasable pen to transfer the design onto your fabric. Place it in the embroidery hoop ready for stitching. Use 3 strands of light green (164) to stitch leaf stitch along the long, thin leaves. Start from the top of each leaf and work downwards, making sure that you cover the lines of the design.

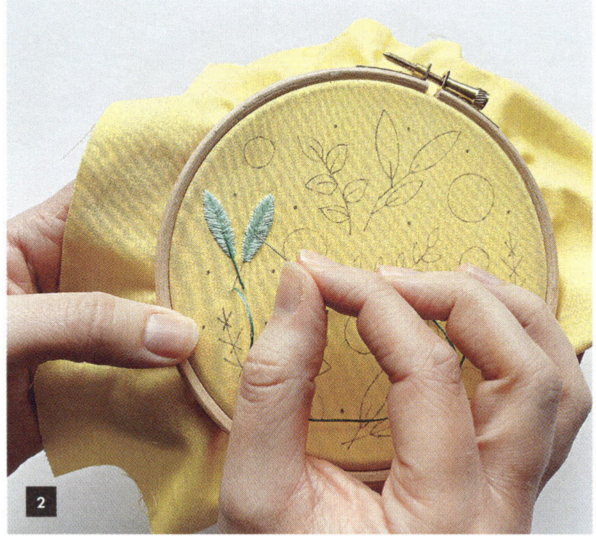
2

3

4

5

2. Add the stem details to the leaves with long straight stitches, using 3 strands of deep water green (3814). Tie off at the back of each stem so that the tension is good, and also to avoid seeing the dark thread through the front of the fabric.

3. Stitch the smaller leaves with vertical satin stitches, using 3 strands of mid deep water green (992).

4. Add the stems to this plant with some small backstitches using light teal (964). When you stitch the stems over the leaves, you might need to stitch over the top again so that they stand out from the satin stitch.

5. Use 3 strands of deep water green (3814) to stitch the thorn stitches. The couched thread will curve as you stitch over the top, so don't worry if it feels too straight at first.

6

7

8

9

6. Stitch the central motif with chained feather stitch in dark deep water green (991). The stems will need to be a little shorter than in the example shown in the stitch guide, as this will help the line to curve more easily.

7. Use a tapestry needle to make a hole in the centre of the eyelet stitches, before stitching with 3 strands of deep water green (3814).

8. Using 3 strands of sand gold (677), stitch five lines on the remaining circles of the design (you can draw the lines on the fabric with your heat erasable pen first if that's helpful). Whip the wheels to complete the stitch.

9. Add French knots to the design, with 3 strands of pale cream thread (746). Wrap the thread around the needle three times each time. When complete, finish the back of the hoop.

polaroid hoop

This versatile project is a brilliant way to mark a celebration or event, and could easily be personalised with additional text for an extra special touch if you wish.

Stitches: brick and cross, straight, arrowhead, double fern, backstitch.

You will need

- An 18cm (7″) embroidery hoop
- A 20 x 22cm (8 x 8½″) piece of DMC 14 count soluble canvas
- 27 x 27cm (11 x 11″) piece of chambray fabric
- Thread - bright purple (3837), dark pink (601), pale pink (605), white (blanc)
- A piece of white felt - a 22 x 22cm (9 x 9″) square will be plenty
- A pencil
- A ruler
- A water erasable pen
- Some pins

This project is something that I've had in my head for ages, and it was great to finally make it. I intended to make it as an anniversary present for my husband a few years ago, so it's better late than never. I had these Polaroid prints made - you can get them really easily online. Simply upload your photos to one of the photo processing websites and they will format your photos into 1970s retro style photo prints with a clean white frame. You could just use a standard print and cut it down to size if you prefer (but bear in mind that you might need to tweak the size of the felt if you do this).

1

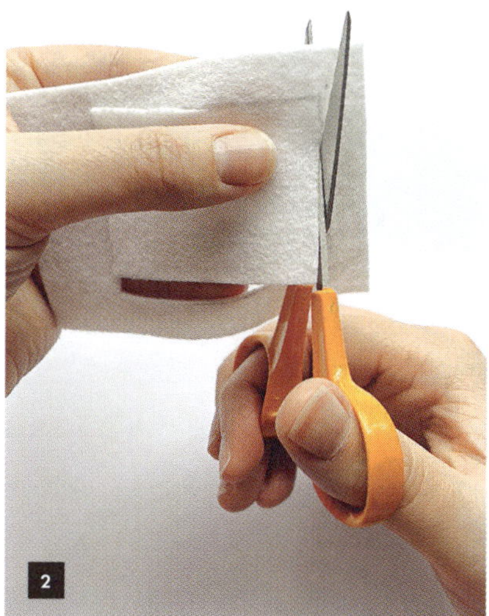
2

INSTRUCTIONS

1. Take one of your Polaroid photos and place it on top of the felt. Measure and cut around it, so that there is roughly ½ cm around each edge. Then cut another piece the same size for the other photo. The finished size for my photos was 10 x 7.2cm.

2. Use a ruler to measure where the hole will be cut out of the middle. The size for my Polaroids was 6.5 x 4.7cm. Use a small, sharp pair of scissors to carefully cut the rectangle out of the centre.

3

4

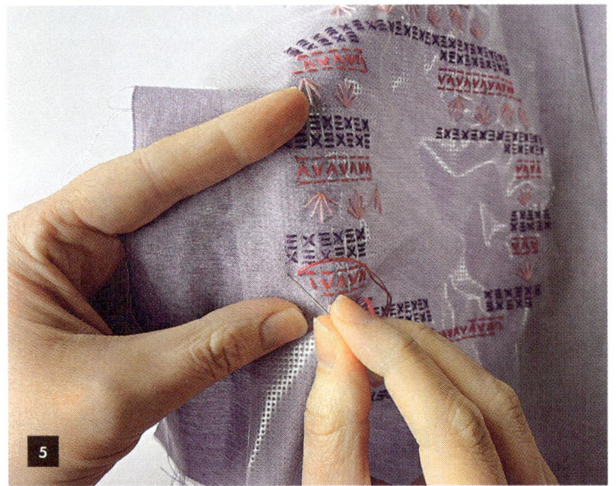
5

6

3. Place your fabric on top of the inner ring of your embroidery hoop. Position the soluble canvas on top, at a slight angle so that the stitches will be on the diagonal. Put the outer ring on top and secure it in position. On the felt, mark the position of the corners of the Polaroid with a water erasable pen.

4. Thread a needle with 3 strands of bright purple (3837). Choose a spot to start on the counted embroidery chart (in the templates section from page 118) and begin with some of the brick and cross sections. Repeat the dark pink (601) for the straight and arrowhead stitches, and the double fern in pale pink (605). You don't need to stitch all the way under the Polaroid, but it's helpful to go a little way in to avoid gaps in the pattern. Keep referring to the pattern as you go.

5. Take the fabric out of the hoop. It's impossible to stitch right the way to the edge of the fabric, so to get the continuous effect you'll need to add the final stitches freehand as shown. Just take your time adding these to the edge of the design.

6. Run a bowl of warm water and submerge the fabric. The canvas will dissolve in the water to reveal

7

8

9

the fabric underneath. You can cut out the excess soluble canvas from the middle to avoid wasting it beforehand if you like (just pop it somewhere for another project!). Leave it somewhere to dry.

7. Thread a needle with 3 strands of white thread. Carefully stitch a line of backstitch down the left hand edge of one of the felt Polaroid pieces, about 2mm from the edge. Put the stitched fabric back in the hoop (paint it beforehand if you want to add a pop of colour). Arrange the felt Polaroid piece on top to make sure you're happy with the position, then pin it in place on the hoop.

8. Continue the line of backstitches around the remaining edges of the Polaroid, to attach it to the fabric in the hoop. Try to keep them a similar size and roughly 2mm or so away from the edge. Then repeat for the other photo, making sure the opening is on the left and that you don't accidentally sew up the first Polaroid. Finish the back of the hoop with some Perle thread.

9. The final thing to do is to pop your chosen photos in their new frames, and then your hoop is ready to display or give as a present.

akvarelmaling
12 farver à 12 ml
12 colours containing 12 ml

stitched wire basket

When it comes to craft supplies, you can never have too much storage! Try your hand at stitching on a completely different material and create something unique.

Stitches: feather, double fern, eyelet, buttonhole wheel.

You will need

- A wire basket
- A selection of Sirdar Happy Cotton balls: Bubblegum (799), Juicy (792), Quack (788), Laundry (782), Bubbly (785), Yacht (786), Currant bun (756)
- A large tapestry or rug needle
- Some small, sharp scissors

One of the things that I really wanted to do in this book was to experiment with different materials to embroider on. I've never used much yarn, but after discovering Sirdar Happy Cotton I know that it will be something that I'm going to work with more. It's beautifully soft and so lovely to stitch with. The array of bright colours is a bonus too! You'll need a long, blunt needle with a large eye for this project, and the most important thing to check is that it actually fits through the holes first.

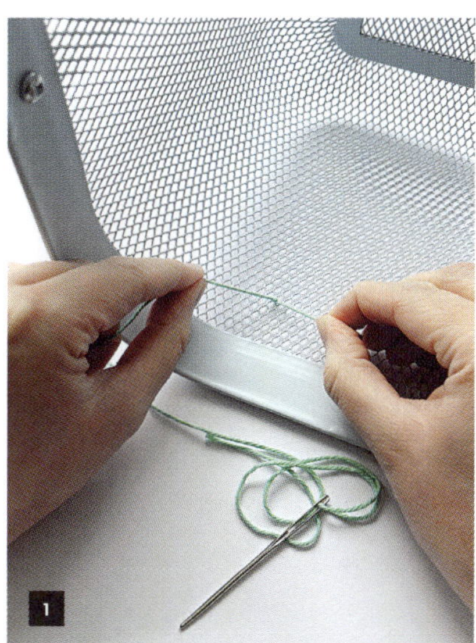
1

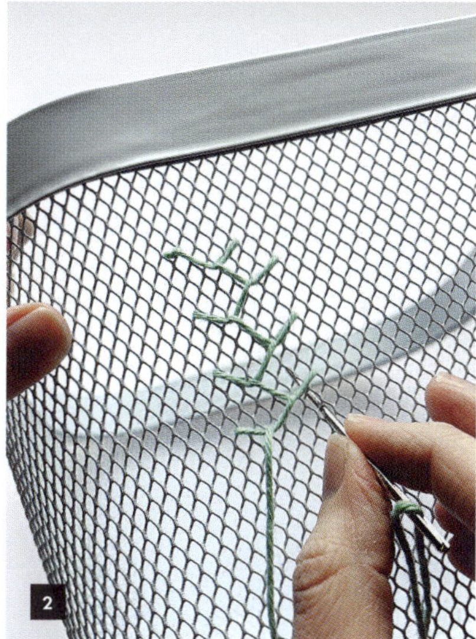
2

INSTRUCTIONS

1. Choose a colour to start with, and cut a generous length of yarn. Starting near to the top of the basket, thread the yarn through one of the holes and then tie a tight double knot at the back to secure it in place.

2. Work to the right of the knot and count four holes along. Push the needle through, and then come up in the centre a couple of rows down to create the first stitch of feather stitch. Continue working the feather stitch to the right of this first stitch and then back again, moving down the basket. Tie securely at the bottom.

3

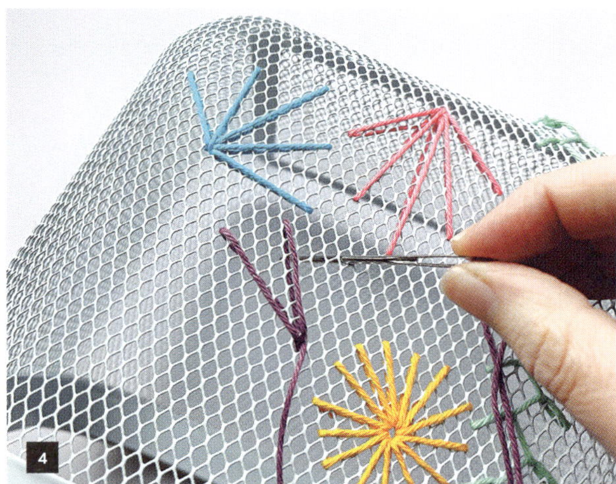
4

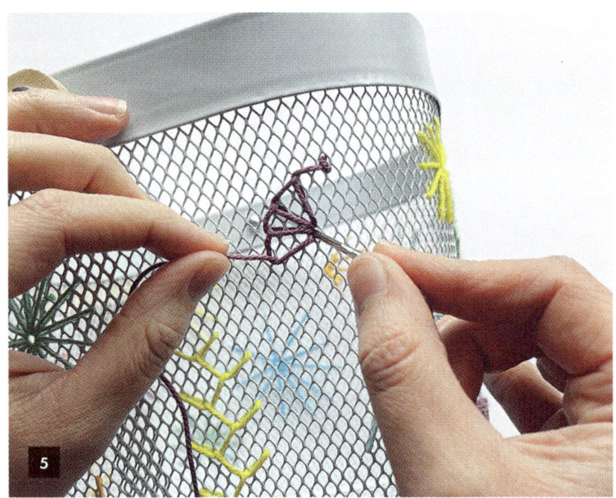
5

3. Choose another colour of yarn and stitch some double fern stitches on the basket, making sure to tie it tightly and trim off any excess. You may wish to try stitching this stitch from the edge to the middle, as that's helpful for tying off at the back. Add eyelet and buttonhole wheels too.

4. Continue stitching a combination of these four stitches in different colours and sizes around the whole basket.

5. When you reach the point where you started, you'll need to plan ahead a little to make sure that the stitches are evenly spaced. Trim off any loose yarn at the back and your basket is ready to use.

chapter 5: textures & knots

The final chapter of stitches in this book is 'textures and knots'. Some of these stitches are simpler than others, and some take a little time to experiment with, but all of them are a wonderful way to add something completely different to your work. Adding new textures into designs can really bring them to life, and I hope you'll love experimenting with these stitches as much as I have.

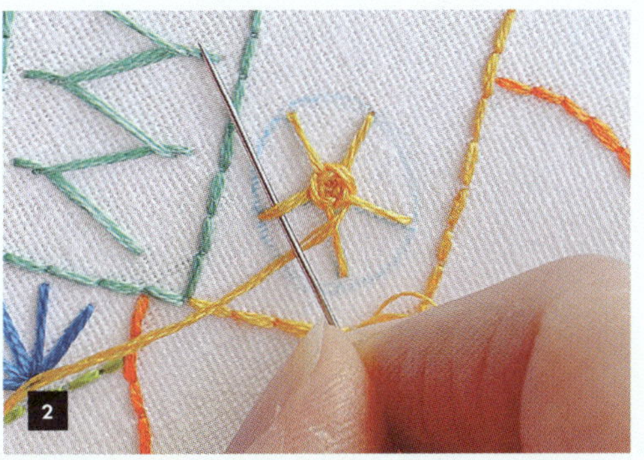

Woven wheel (53)

1. Draw a five-spoked wheel onto the fabric. Stitch the spokes with straight stitches, working from the edge to the centre. Come up through the fabric as close as you can to the centre.

2. Take the working thread over the first spoke and then weave it under the second. Repeat, alternating over and under each spoke around the wheel until you reach the outer edge. Remove any visible pen lines when complete.

Danish knot (54)

1. Come up through the fabric and go back down diagonally to the right. Pull through to make a small, diagonal straight stitch. Come back up through the fabric at a point which creates the third tip of a small triangle.

2. Come over the top of the straight stitch and then underneath it, without going through the fabric. Pull the needle through, making sure it goes over the top of the working thread. Be careful not to pull too tightly. Repeat once more, and then push your needle back through the bottom left corner to finish.

Square boss (55)

1. Stitch two diagonal stitches to make a cross. Come back up next to the centre, and take the thread over one diagonal to make a small straight stitch over the top.

2. Repeat on the other sides, making sure that the next straight stitch goes into the previous one (as with backstitch). When you have a square in the centre, tie off the thread at the back.

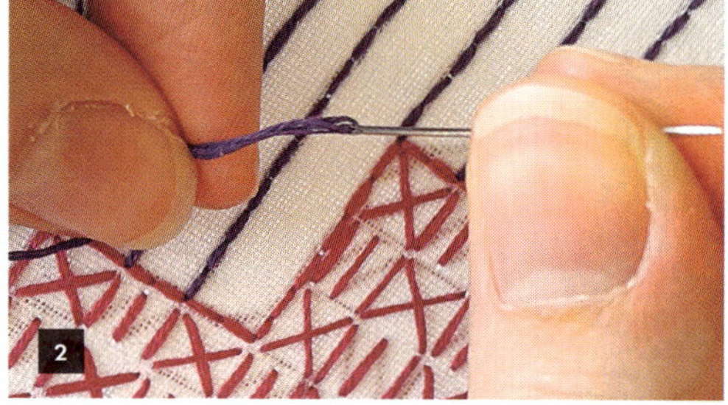

Bullion knot (56)

1. Come up through the fabric, and go back down 1cm or so further along. Then come back up exactly where the first stitch started, leaving a large loop of the working thread on top of the fabric. Carefully wrap this working thread around your needle (roughly 10 times or so), being careful not to pull it too tightly or leave it too loose.

2. Move the wound thread to the bottom of your needle, and then gently pull it through completely. Push the needle back through the fabric at the other end of the stitch, and tie off at the back.

Long and short (57)

1. At one end of the section to be stitched, stitch a long straight stitch followed by another half the length right next to it. Continue until the end of the section.

2. Fill in the gaps with the shorter stitches with long stitches the same size as the ones in the first row. Keep working along in this way until you reach the end. At the other end, you should finish with a row of long and short stitches.

Padded satin (58)
1. Fill the area to be stitched with small straight stitches in any direction. For extra padded texture, stitch more straight stitches over the top to build up the coverage.

2. Stitch satin stitch over the top, filling in the gaps as you go to create a smooth finish. Make sure that all of the stitches underneath are completely covered with satin stitch.

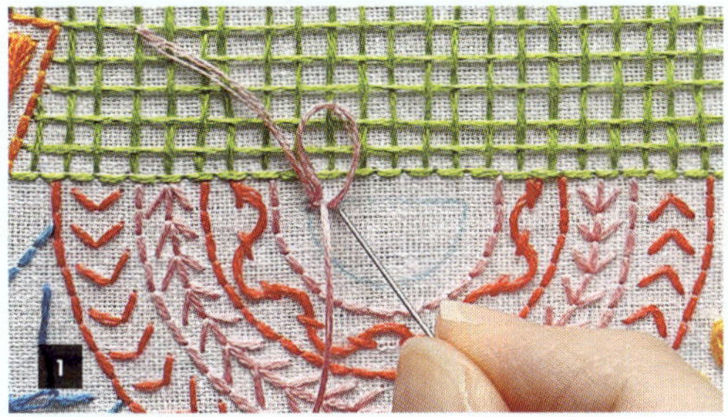

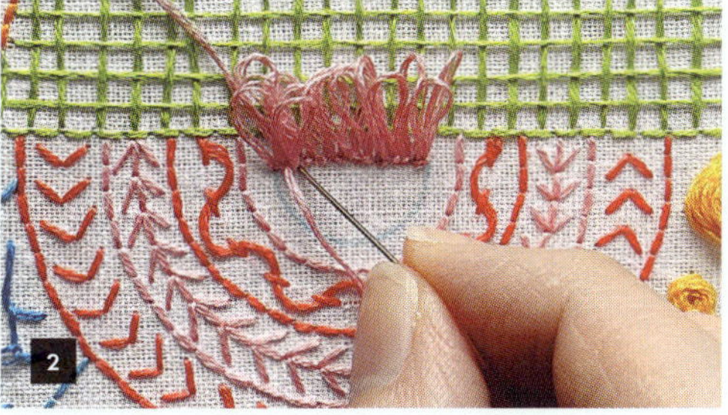

Turkey (59)
1. Take your needle down through the fabric where you want the first stitch to be. Anchor it in with a small straight stitch at the bottom. Come back up through the fabric. Create a small loop of thread by pushing the needle through very close to where you came up. Leave the loop loose, and anchor it with another small straight stitch.
2. Repeat, continuing to make loops which cover the area to be stitched. When the area is covered, trim the loops to the desired length. Remove any loose pieces of thread from your work.

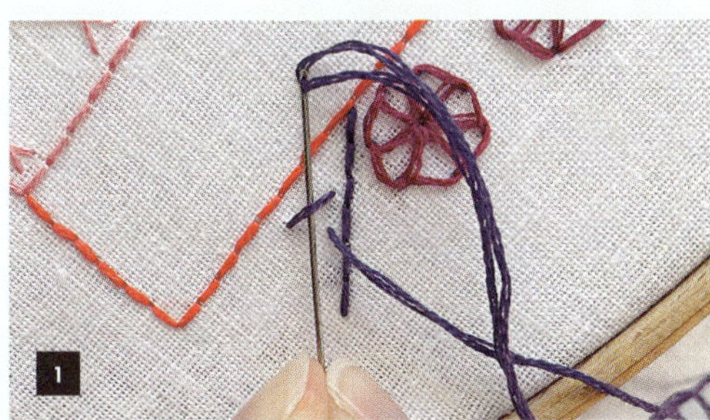

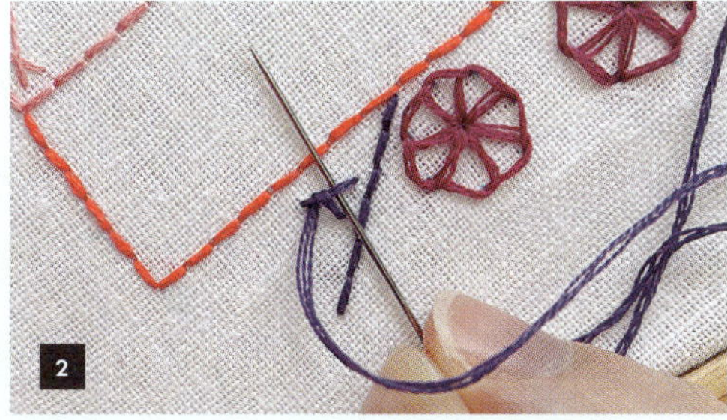

Palestrina (60)
1. Come up through the fabric in the bottom left corner of an imaginary square, pushing it through at the top right corner. Come back at the bottom right corner. Take the needle underneath the diagonal stitch from top to bottom, without going through the fabric. Pull through gently. **2.** Take the needle over the bottom right corner and push it under the stitch close to the top right corner. Push the needle back through the fabric in the top left corner to finish the cross stitch. Tie off.

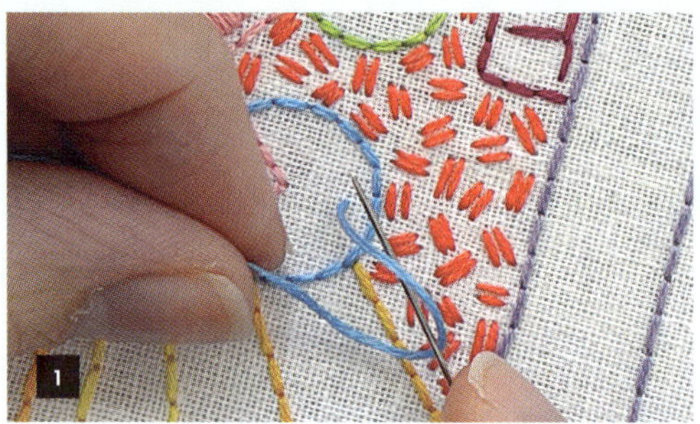

Colonial knot (61)

1. Come up through the fabric where you'd like the finished knot to be. Make a small loop with the working thread and take the needle through it. Wrap the working thread over the top of the needle to the left of the loop, creating what looks like a figure of 8.

2. Push your needle through the fabric close to where you came out. Tighten the thread around your needle and then pull it through to create the knot.

Ring knot (62)

1. Come up through the fabric where you'd like the finished knot to be. Wrap the working thread loosely around the needle twice.

2. Push your needle through the fabric close to where you came out. Tighten the thread around your needle a little (but not completely) and then pull it through to create the knot.

Loop (63)

1. Draw a line to be stitched with an erasable pen. Come up at the end of the line, and push it back through the fabric a little way along, leaving a small loop. Stitch another similar loop to the right and in front of the first.

2. Repeat along the line to be stitched, and then gently tie off the thread at the back. You can use a needle to rearrange the last few loops if you've tied a little too tightly.

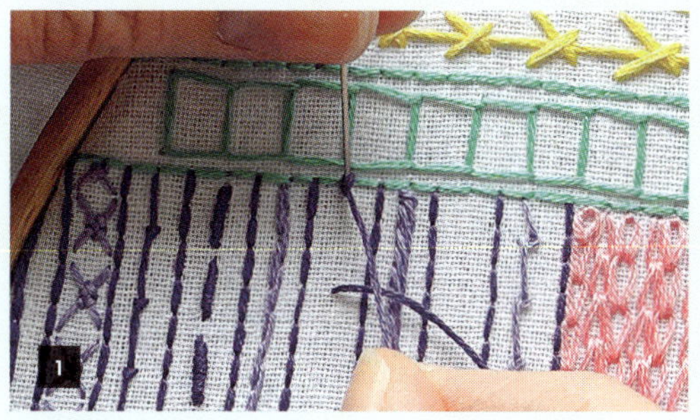

Cast on (64)

1. Make a 1cm stitch, leaving a large loop of thread instead of pulling through. Come back up where you started. Make a small loop and wrap it over the needle, pulling it to the bottom of the needle.

2. Add more loops in the same way, keeping tension consistent. When stitches cover the length, gently pull your needle through. Push your needle back through the other end of the stitch, and tie off at the back.

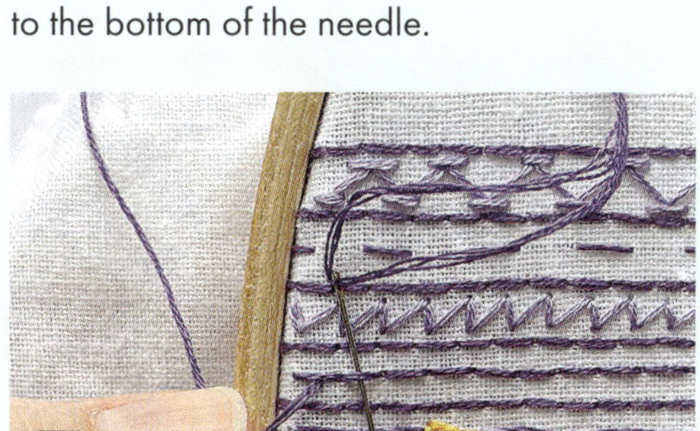

Forbidden (65)

1. Stitch a line of backstitches. Come up through the middle of the last stitch without piercing it, then push the needle underneath the top of the next stitch, leaving a loop of thread.

2. Take the needle underneath the first backstitch and over the loop. Leave another loop, before repeating this process with the next stitch and along the line.

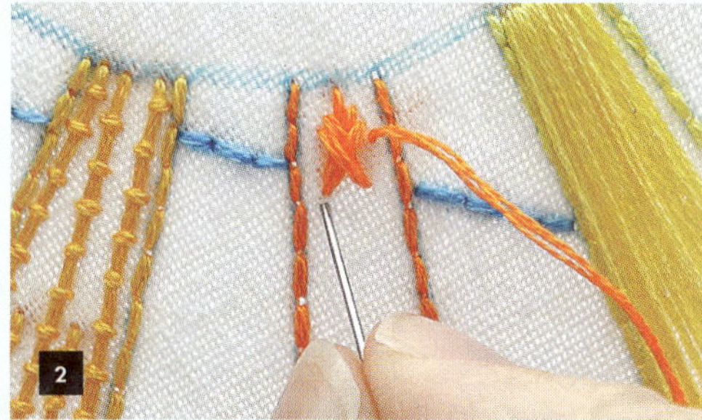

Fishbone (66)

1. Stitch a vertical straight stitch in the centre of one end of the section to be stitched. Come up through the fabric near to the top, but diagonally down and right a little. Push it back through the fabric a little further down from the first stitch and diagonally to the left.

2. Stitch a similar stitch in a mirror image, so you create a cross over the first two stitches. Continue stitching in this way as required, following the outline of the area to be stitched.

Brick (67)

1. Stitch a line of large backstitches down the centre of the area to be stitched, keeping the stitches the same size. Stitch another line right next to the first, but slightly off-centre to create the brick effect.

2. The next line above should be stitched to match placement of the stitches in the first, to make sure that it is neat. Repeat as required.

Crown (68)

1. Come up through the fabric, and go down roughly 1 cm or so to the side. Come back up through the bottom of the loop, pulling the working thread gently to create a large scallop stitch. Create a small straight stitch at the bottom.

2. Add two more straight stitches either side, leaving a gap in between them and pointing the outer ones out diagonally. Tie off at the back.

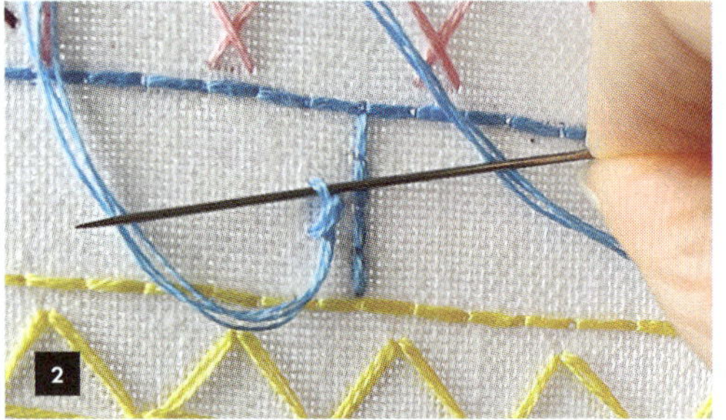

Pearl (69)

1. Come up through the fabric at one end of the line. Using the sewing method, take the needle down and through again, to the left and either side of the line, pulling the needle through to create a diagonal stitch. Take your needle and push it underneath the stitch right to left, without going through the fabric.

2. Take the needle under the stitch right to left again, moving it over the working thread when you pull it through gently to make the knot. Repeat as required along the line.

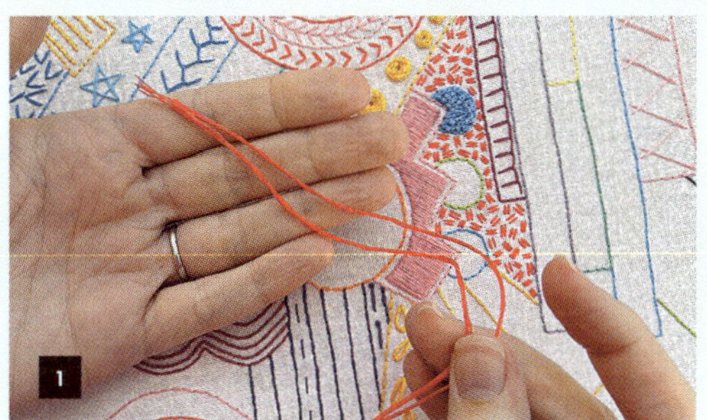

1

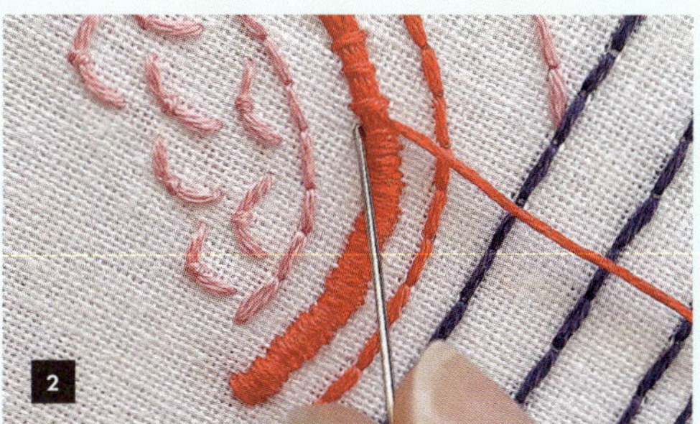

2

Satin couching (70)

1. Thread a needle with 6 strands of thread, and tie a knot in one end. Come up through the fabric and then remove the needle. Add another similar couched thread if you wish.

2. Thread the needle with 3 strands of the same colour thread. Bring it up through the fabric at the end of the couched thread. Make a small straight stitch over the top. Repeat along the line, making sure the couched threads are completely covered. Tie off all threads at the back when complete.

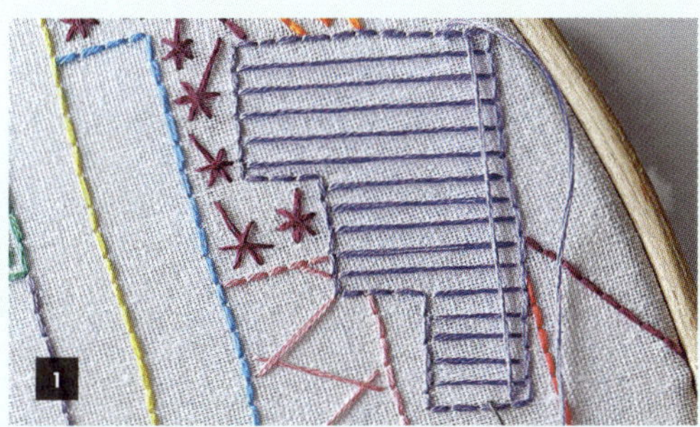

1

2

Trellis (71)

1. Stitch a series of horizontal straight stitches from one side of the area to the other. Stitch vertical stitches over the top of the horizontal ones, making sure they are evenly spaced too.

2. Where each horizontal and vertical stitch meet, stitch a small diagonal straight stitch to secure. Repeat until the whole section is covered, keeping stitches the same size and in the same direction throughout.

1

2

Weave (72)

1. Stitch a series of straight stitches from one side of the area to the other, keeping them evenly spaced.

2. Come up through the fabric and weave the thread over the first straight stitch and then under the next, repeating along the line. Repeat alternately as required.

BLOOM

bloom hoop

This negative space embroidery has a unique little twist, with the addition of the teal coloured fabric in the gaps of the lettering that contrast with the background fabric.

Stitches: long and short, satin, leaf, padded satin, straight, woven wheel, French knots.

You will need

- A 15cm (6") embroidery hoop
- A 18cm (7") embroidery hoop to stitch in
- 27 x 27cm (11 x 11") piece of lime green fabric
- A 12 x 2.5cm (5 x 1") piece of teal fabric
- A 12 x 2.5cm (5 x 1") piece of Bondaweb
- A black Sublime Stitching transfer pen
- Some vellum paper to transfer the design in reverse (scan the QR code on page 118 to download the reverse templates)
- An iron
- Thread - light red (3705), light orange (722), pale gold (17), lime green (16), bright sea green (959), bright blue (3846), light purple (340), mid bright rose (961), light rose pink (3716)

I'm a huge fan of negative space embroidery. I just love the texture and the technique involved in creating the text by stitching a variety of elements around it. The design was inspired by a 'Joy' hoop that I created for Workshop Week in 2022, a week of online art workshops (@theworkshopweek). It's a project that I started at my old studio and shop, which sadly I had to move out of later that year. I have hugely mixed emotions about having to leave my space, but this hoop is a symbol of moving forward, hope and flourishing.

INSTRUCTIONS

1. Carefully trace the design onto the vellum paper in reverse. If you don't have a Sublime Stitching pen, I'd recommend using a heat erasable pen as an alternative - but you'll need to start at step 2 instead.

2. Attach the small piece of teal fabric to the centre of the lime fabric with Bondaweb. Follow manufacturer's instructions and use the hoop as a guide to positioning. Carefully position the vellum paper the right way up on top of the fabric so the text fits into the teal gap. Iron on the design with a cool iron (or draw on with a heat pen if you're using this method instead).

3. Begin the stitching by starting with the rainbow section. Thread a needle with 3 strands of light red (3705), and stitch a line of long and short stitches at the end of the top section of the rainbow as shown. Work around any floral elements that intersect the rainbow, stitching up to the lines, but not over them. Add the remaining colours in a similar way.

4. Stitch the sun with 3 strands of pale gold (17) ensuring that the stitches of the central sun section are slightly on the diagonal. Work each of the sun rays vertically from the middle, using satin stitch too.

5. The pink daisies are next to be stitched, and are also stitched using satin stitch. Use 3 strands of mid bright rose (961) for the petals of the large and two

smallest ones, with the medium sized daisies in the light rose pink (3716). Add contrasting straight stitches over the petals in the contrasting pink.

6. Add leaf stitch to the outer leaves top left and bottom right, with 3 strands of bright sea green (959). The leaf in the top middle should be stitched in lime green (16) for contrast.

7. Stitch the hearts with a combination of satin and padded satin stitch, keeping the stitches horizontal throughout. Then add the heart-shaped flowers by stitching the middle section in pale gold (17) using a satin stitch. Use light rose pink (3716) to satin stitch the petals, working them vertically to add texture.

8. Add the woven wheels in light purple (340). You'll need to be very careful not to catch the other stitches with your needle as you work these wheels.

9. Add the French knots to the daisies for the final touch, and the negative space will really come to life here. Use pale gold (17), and wrap the thread around the needle three times each time.

CHOC TRIANGLES
BON BONS
TOFFEES
CHERRY STICKS
CARAMELS
FRUIT LOLLIES
MARSH MALLOWS
FRIED EGGS

sweet shop hoop

This fun, textural hoop uses a variety of stitches - it will take you back to your childhood with some classic pick 'n' mix sweets in the old-style sweetie jars. Yum!

Stitches: backstitch, long and short, Danish knot, ring knot, sheaf, bullion knots, square boss, woven wheel, straight, cast on, colonial knot, whipped backstitch, satin.

You will need

- A 15cm (6") embroidery hoop
- 22 x 22cm (9 x 9") piece of white Essex linen fabric
- A fine tip water erasable pen and brush pen
- Thread - dark beaver grey (844), dark bright green (3850), pale pink (605), dark cornflower (792), bright red (666), light tangerine (742), bright green (907), bright yellow (444), bright orange (970), pearl grey (415), off-white (3865), light kingfisher (996), pale gold (17), lime green (16), bubblegum pink (956),
- Colour Variations thread in brown mix (4145) and pastel mix (4160)

When I first learnt how to stitch a Danish knot, my immediate thought was that they reminded me of those Quality Street green chocolate triangles. Maybe I was hungry at the time, but I haven't been able to look at one since without thinking about those sweets. When I thought about it, a lot of embroidery knots look a bit like sweets, so that became the inspiration for the design for this hoop. Fried eggs are my favourites, and I think that the stitched ones here might just be the cutest thing I've ever stitched.

1

INSTRUCTIONS

1. Trace the design onto the fabric with a fine tip water erasable pen. Place the fabric in the hoop so you're ready to stitch. Outline the jars using 2 strands of dark beaver grey (844), stitching small backstitches all the way around the jar and the neck.

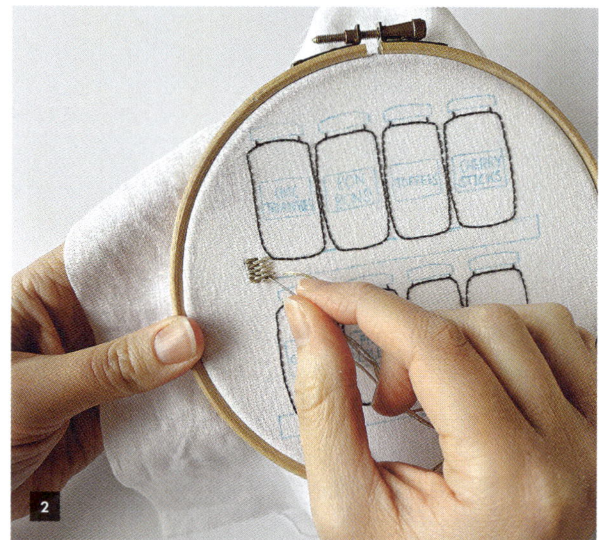
2

3

3a

3b

2. Thread a needle with 6 strands of the brown Colour Variations thread (4145). Stitch long and short stitches across both shelves, and the thread will naturally create a wood effect as you go.

3. Now for the fun bit - adding the sweets to the jars! You can fill up the jars as much as you like, but having a mix of levels in the jars gives a more authentic look. Stitch using the following colours and stitches:

Chocolate triangles - dark bright green (3850), Danish knot
Bon bons - pale pink (605), ring knot
Toffees - dark cornflower (792), sheaf
Cherry sticks - bright red (666), bullion knot
Caramels - light tangerine (742), square boss
Fruit lollies - mix of bright green (907), bright yellow (444), bright orange (970) and bright red (666), woven wheels; pearl grey (415) for sticks, straight

Marshmallows - Colour Variations pastel mix (4160), cast on
Fried eggs - bright yellow (444), colonial knot yolks; off-white (3865) for edges, whipped backstitch

4. Thread your needle with 2 strands of dark beaver grey (844) to outline the jar labels with backstitch. Use 1 strand of the same colour for the text, and stitch tiny backstitches in the direction of the text.

5. Add extra colour to the jar lids using small, vertical satin stitches, using 3 strands of thread, in light kingfisher (996), pale gold (17), lime green (16) and bubblegum pink (956).

6. Remove any visible pen lines with the brush pen. Then place in a painted hoop and finish the back so it's ready to display.

WE DON'T MAKE MISTAKES
JUST HAPPY LITTLE ACCIDENTS
WATER COLOUR
Crimson Red 12ml e 0.4US fl.oz
Ultramarine Blue 12ml e 0.4US fl.oz
Cerulean Blue 12ml e 0.4US fl.oz

happy little accidents hoop

This hoop is perfect for any artist, not just stitchers! It's a wonderful reminder to keep exploring and creating, and that making mistakes is an important part of the process.

Stitches: satin couching, padded satin, weave, colonial knot, long and short, trellis, ring knot, brick, cast on, fishbone, satin, turkey, whipped backstitch.

You will need

- An 18cm (7″) embroidery hoop
- A piece of white felt, 14 x 12cm (5½ x 4¾″)
- A piece of Bondaweb, 14 x 12cm (5½ x 4¾″)
- A pencil
- An iron
- 27 x 27cm (11 x 11″) piece of light blue fabric
- A heat erasable pen
- Thread - dark turquoise (3808), magenta (917), dark watermelon (3801), light orange (722), yellow (726), bright green (907), teal (3851), light kingfisher (996), ocean blue (824), dark violet (3746), light silver (03), medium brown (433), light brown (434), very light brown (435), tan (436), dark navy blue (823)

When I started The Happy Stitch Project, my friend Louise said that the videos reminded her of the American artist Bob Ross. She thought my voice was relaxing to listen to as I demonstrated the stitches, just like Bob! He was famous for the many quotes that he dropped into conversation as he was painting, and I decided to stitch this one, as it's her favourite. So this hoop is for Louise, to celebrate all those little creative mistakes that we've made along the way, and how much we've learnt from them and from each other.

1

INSTRUCTIONS

1. Trace the paint palette shape onto the smooth side of the Bondaweb. Iron it onto the white felt, following the manufacturer's instructions. Carefully cut it out with some small, sharp scissors. Position the paint palette shape on the light blue fabric, and iron in position.

2. Trace the rest of the design onto the fabric with the heat erasable pen, lining up the palette first. If you need a printable version, scan the QR code on page 118 for a template. Then pop it in the hoop so you're ready to stitch.

3. Thread a needle with 6 strands of dark turquoise (3808). Stitch several couching threads along the length of the first paintbrush. Then use 3 strands of the same colour to satin couch across them. Repeat with the second brush using magenta (917).

4. Add the paint splodges to the palette using a variety of textural stitches. You'll need to stitch them close together to give the effect of colour blocks on the palette. Use the following colours and stitches:

Dark violet (3746), weave stitch
Ocean blue (824), colonial knot
Light kingfisher (996), long and short
Teal (3851), trellis
Bright green (907), ring knot
Yellow (726), brick
Light orange (722), cast on
Dark watermelon (3801), fishbone

5. To stitch the brush bristles, start by stitching vertical satin stitches to cover the outline. Use 3 strands of a

mix of brown shades, starting with the darkest ones (433 and 434) to give a natural effect.

6. Add some long turkey stitches to the bristles, making sure that they cover the satin stitching underneath. Secure them with very small anchor stitches to keep them as hidden as possible. Use 3 strands again, with a mixture of the brown thread in shades 433, 434, 435 and add the lighter tan (436) too.

7. When the turkey stitching is complete, trim the loops and then cut the thread to the desired length, making sure that there is a clear shape to the brush bristles when finished.

8. Add the final brush details using 3 strands of light silver thread (03). For this section, stitch a padded satin stitch. Start by adding lots of straight stitches to fill in the area, and add extra on the blue fabric so it will be level with the felt palette. Then add satin stitches over the top in the same direction as the rest of the brush that you stitched earlier.

9. Stitch very small backstitches over the lettering using 2 strands of dark navy blue thread (823). You can either leave them or whip the backstitches if you'd like the text to be a little bolder. Place the design in a painted hoop, and check that you're happy with positioning before finishing the back.

Brighter days are coming

brighter days 3D scene

If you want to take your stitching to the next level, then this project is for you. Create a 3D scene with embroidery, using a combination of subtle and bold textures.

Stitches: palestrina, forbidden, pearl, crown, backstitch, straight, running, loop, whipped backstitch, blanket.

You will need

- A piece of yellow felt, 18 x 18cm (7 x 7") plus another piece big enough to fit the sun template
- A piece of white felt, 18 x 18cm (7 x 7")
- Thread - yellow (726), medium yellow (743), black (310), white (blanc), bubblegum pink (956), light salmon (761)
- A water erasable pen and brush pen
- A heat erasable pen (optional)
- A 12cm (5") embroidery hoop for stitching in
- A small piece of pale pink felt, big enough for two banners to be cut out
- Some small pieces of Plasticard (one A4 sheet will be more than enough)
- Craft scissors
- 1.5mm craft wire in gold and silver
- Wire cutters
- Some Superglue (or something suitable for using on felt and plastic)
- A cork coaster
- A craft knife and cutting mat
- A 19cm (7½") glass dome and base

This project is a reworking of a hoop that I designed as a kit to accompany The Happy Stitch Project. The 'Brighter Days' hoop was designed in early 2021 when we were in the second Covid-19 lockdown, and I wanted to stitch something really positive to help get through those tough winter months. It felt right to adapt this design for a 3D scene, and true to form it was one of my experiments when I created it. I'm so happy with the result, and I hope that you love stitching it too.

1

2

INSTRUCTIONS

1. Trace the sun design onto the yellow felt using a water erasable pen. Always do a spot test of the felt first to make sure that the pen can be easily removed. Once traced, place it in the embroidery hoop so you're ready for stitching.

2. Stitch a variety of different stitches along the sunbeams, using 3 strands of thread. Start one sunbeam from the left with palestrina (726), then forbidden (743), then pearl (726) and crown (743). Once complete, stitch the outer sunbeams too - the left will be crown (726) and the right palestrina (743).

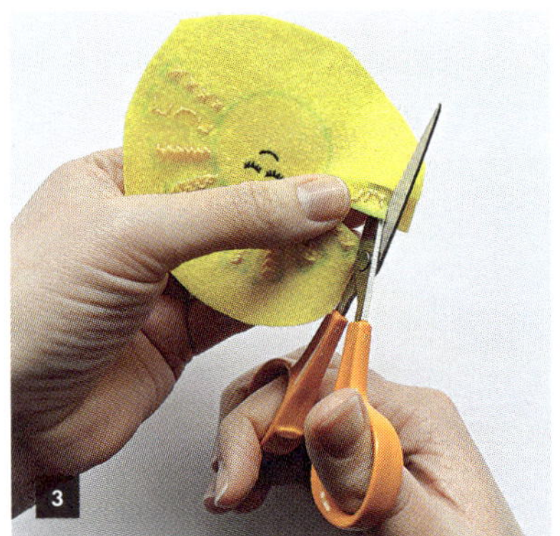
3

4

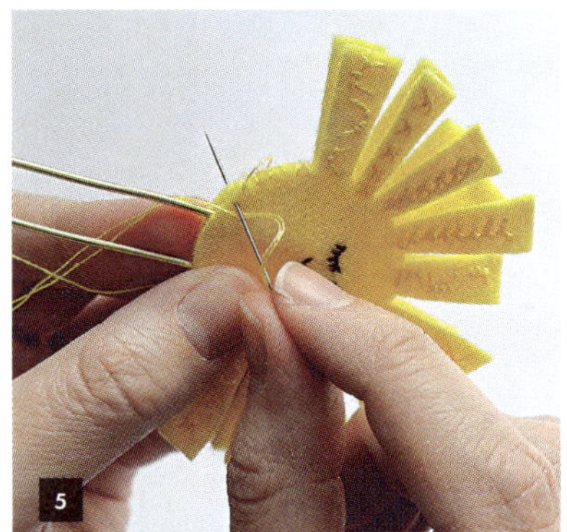
5

6

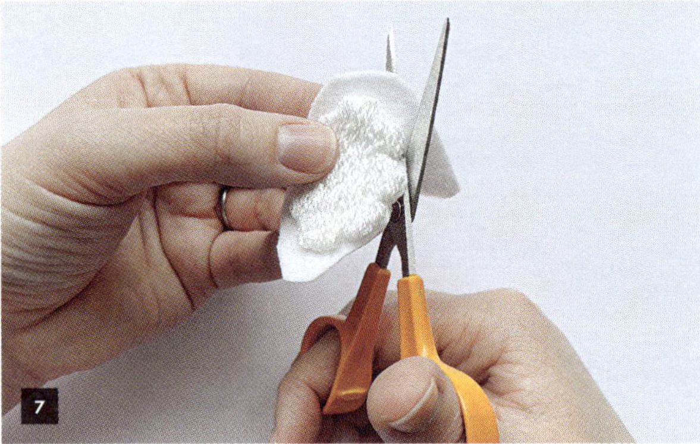
7

3. Using 2 strands of black (310), stitch tiny backstitches to create the eyes and mouth of the sun. The eyelashes are created using very small straight stitches. Make sure you tie off at the back of each eye, just to avoid black thread being visible from the front. Use a small, sharp pair of scissors to trim around the design. Then cut out another sun-shaped piece from the smaller piece of yellow felt. Remove any visible pen lines with your water brush, and leave it to dry.

4. Cut two 12cm pieces of gold wire, and a small circle of Plasticard that will fit inside the round section of the sun. Place the unstitched sun shape on a flat surface with the Plasticard on top. Work out where the wires will be positioned (1-2cm in) and then glue in place on the Plasticard. Leave to dry completely.

5. Take the stitched sun shape and place it face up on top of the back piece, with the Plasticard and wire sandwiched in the middle. Using 1 strand of yellow thread (726), stitch a tiny blanket stitch around the circular section of the sun. The sunbeams are fiddly to stitch, so add a small amount of glue to stick each one together and then leave to dry completely.

6. Trace the cloud shapes onto the white felt, and then place it in the embroidery hoop ready for stitching. Thread a needle with 3 strands of white, and then stitch a small running stitch along the outline of the cloud. Fill the area with tightly packed loop stitches. Repeat until the three clouds are complete.

7. Use a small, sharp pair of scissors to cut around the cloud shape, leaving 1mm around the edge so the stitches don't fall out. Cut matching white felt cloud shapes from the remnants of the felt, and cut oval

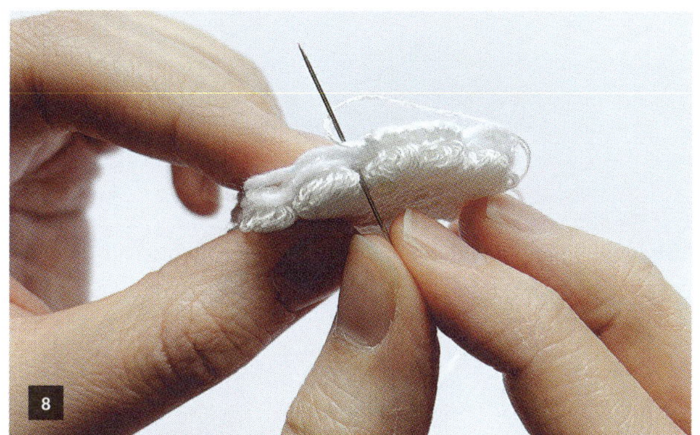

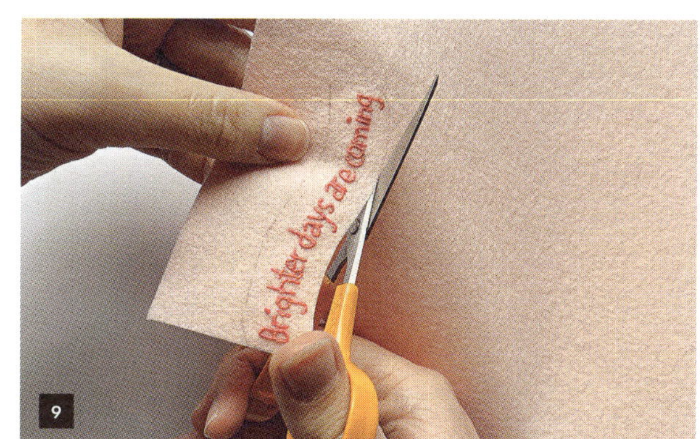

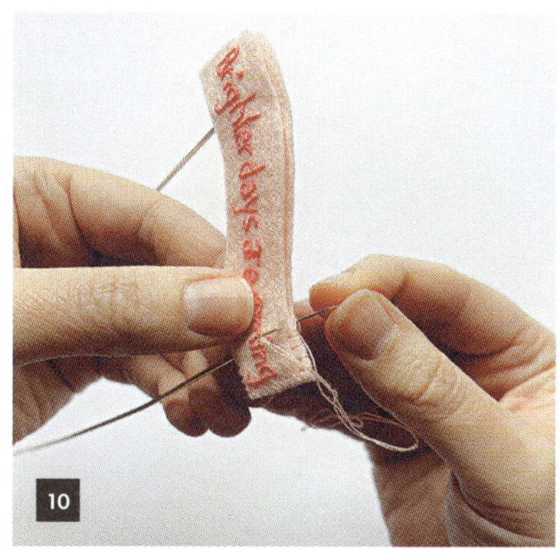

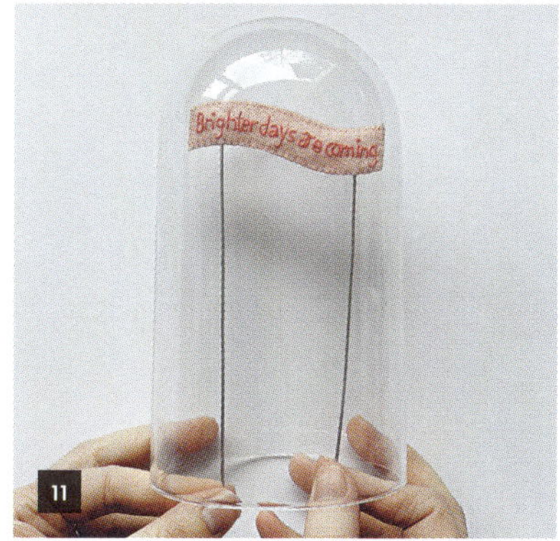

Plasticard shapes to fit inside. Cut one 12cm length of silver wire for each cloud, and then glue as you did with the sun. Leave to dry completely.

8. Take a stitched cloud shape and position it face up on top of the back piece, with the Plasticard and wire sandwiched between the layers. Thread a needle with 2 strands of white and stitch a small blanket stitch around the edge to join the pieces together.

9. Trace the banner shape and text onto the pale pink felt. Stitch the text using 2 strands of bubblegum pink (956), with a whipped backstitch. Cut out the banner shape and trace another banner shape onto the felt and cut that out too along with a small piece of Plasticard to fit inside. Cut two 16cm pieces of silver wire, and glue one at each end of the banner.

10. Put the banner pieces together, with the wire and Plasticard in the middle. Stitch a small blanket stitch around the edges using 1 strand of light salmon (761).

11. Take the banner, and place it inside the glass dome to roughly measure the height. Trim the wire, remembering that less is more. Use a craft knife to trim the coaster to fit the base and dome. Work out the desired position of the banner, using the wires as a guide. Use a pin and a scrap of wire to make two holes in the cork coaster, and slot the banner in place.

12. Repeat with the remaining stitched pieces, making sure to use the wires as a guide so you get the holes in the right place. It is helpful to remove the banner when inserting the clouds, just to help with balance. Once all the stitched pieces are in position, put the coaster on the base, the glass on top, and it's ready to display.

WILD

wild hoop

Add a fun, distinctive twist to turkey stitch with this leopard print design. This stitch gives a wonderful, tactile texture and it's fun to experiment with it in this hoop.

Stitches: turkey.

You will need

- 22 x 22cm (9 x 9") cream or off-white fabric
- A 15cm (6") embroidery hoop for stitching in
- A 12cm (5") embroidery hoop to display the stitching
- Sublime stitching pen and transfer paper
- An iron
- A heat erasable pen
- Thread - light sky blue (3761), lemon (445), pale lilac (211), mint (955), dark steel grey (414), off-white (3865)
- 3 needles

Of all of the new-to-me stitches that I learnt in The Happy Stitch Project, I think turkey stitch has to be my favourite. It's just so tactile, and I love to use it for lettering because it really makes it pop. This is not a quick project to stitch, but it is a lovely one to have on the go and keep dipping in and out of. I was generous with the size of the loops because I wasn't sure what the leopard print would need - but you don't need to stitch them this long.

1

INSTRUCTIONS

1. Trace the design in reverse onto the transfer paper (see QR code on page 118 for the link to download). Trace the edges of the letters and the black shapes, but leave the rest. Transfer onto the fabric, and then use the heat erasable pen to shade in the grey areas on the design, and outline the white sections so that they are clear. Place the fabric in the larger hoop for stitching.

2

3

4

4a

5

2. Thread a needle with 3 strands of light sky blue (3761) and start stitching a turkey stitch in the top left-hand corner of the letter 'w'. Make sure that you secure the stitches with small anchor stitches, and keep them all close together. Stop where you meet the section of white in the top right corner.

3. Thread another needle with 3 strands of off-white thread (3865), and repeat step 2 with this colour. The next line of stitching begins with the dark steel grey (414), so anchor in this colour and stitch along the dark section. At this point, it's helpful to stitch the whole of the darker section before moving on. This enables you to tie off each colour, rather than having 3 working threads on the fabric simultaneously which can get a little confusing.

4. Continue stitching the lettering in this way, changing the colours according to the pattern. For the remaining letters, use lemon (445) for the 'i', pale lilac (211) for the 'l' and mint (955) for the 'd'. Try to resist the urge to cut the loops before all the lettering is stitched, as it will fluff up the ends of the thread.

5. Trim the loops with a small, sharp pair of scissors. I find it helpful to cut the loops by inserting the scissors through the loop and trimming afterwards, but you can just cut the tops off if you prefer. Trim to an even length. Take your time with this part. Place the stitching in the smaller hoop, which can be painted if you wish. Use the closed blades of a small pair of scissors to neaten the lettering. Finish the back, and then tidy up any of the stitches that may have moved out of place.

guides & templates

Here is my guide to finishing the back of your hoop. For years I've been using the same method, because I love to see all the work that has gone into the stitching at the back of the hoop. Here's how I finish my hoops:

1. Place your finished stitching in your hoop, and double-check to make sure you're happy with the position. Tighten the screw with a screwdriver. Trim any excess fabric so you have roughly 2.5cm (1") around the edge.

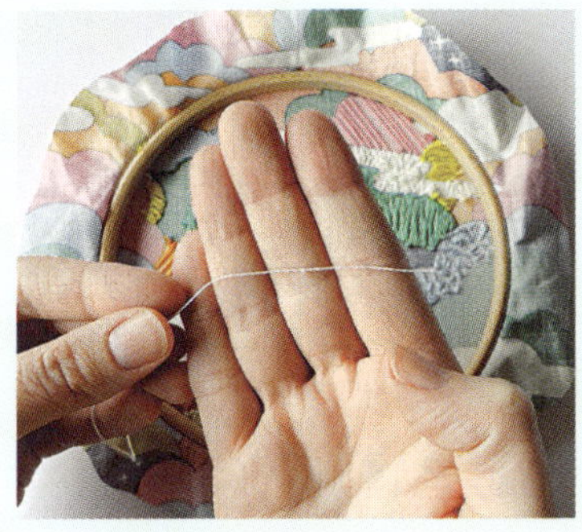

2. Take a length of no.8 perle thread, making sure it's slightly longer than the circumference of your hoop. Tie a double knot in the end but don't trim the excess. Thread the other end onto a needle.

3. Starting at the top of the hoop, fold the excess fabric over and push your needle down and back up through the it. Pull the thread through to the knot.

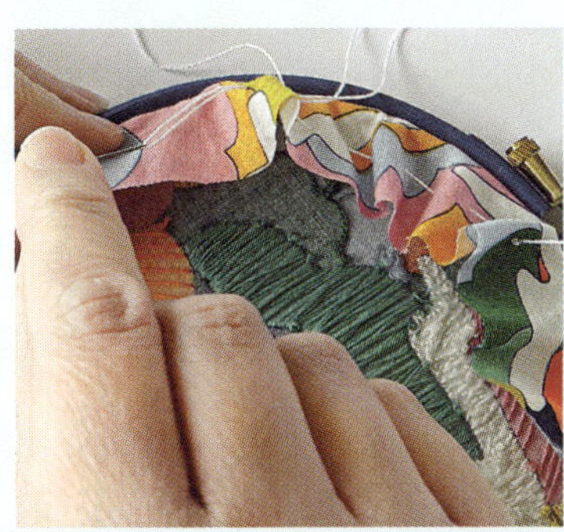

4. Repeat this running stitch around the hoop. As you pull the thread, the fabric will gather together.

5. Tie a double knot (plus one for luck) when you get back to the top of the hoop. Trim off any excess thread with a small, sharp pair of scissors.

6. Ta-dah! The back is finished and your hoop is ready to display.

The Sampler Page 8
60%

http://hellohooray.com/modern-embroidery-handbook/

Cat Nap Hoop Page 16
100% Actual size 152.7mm x 152.7mm

Love Yourself Tee Page 24
100%. Actual size 64.4mm x 64.9mm

LOVE
YOUR
SELF

Botanical Hoop Page 80
100%. Actual size 127mm 127mm

Shelfie Bookmark Page 52
100% Actual size 45mm x 196.8mm

Cuppa Hoop Page 32
100% Actual size 203.2mm x 203.2mm

Sort-of Mandala Hoop Page 60
100% Actual size 177.8mm x 177.8mm

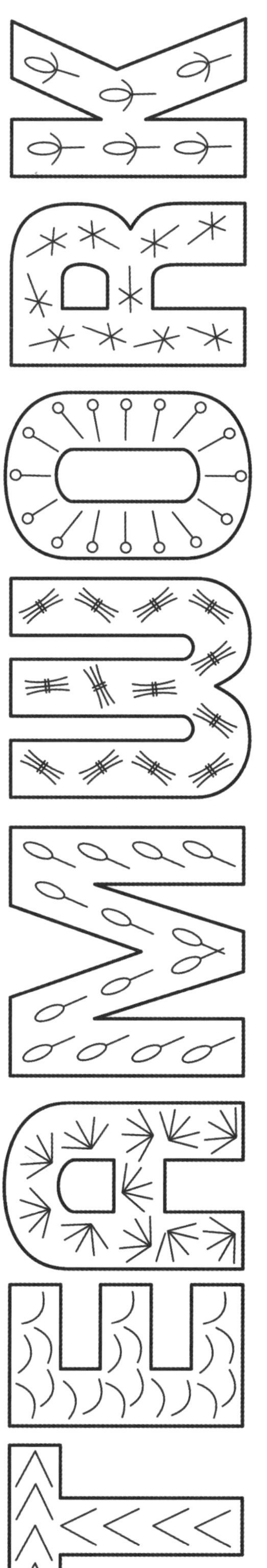

DREAM WORK

Stitched Framed Print
Page 76 100%
Actual size
119.5mm x 262.8mm

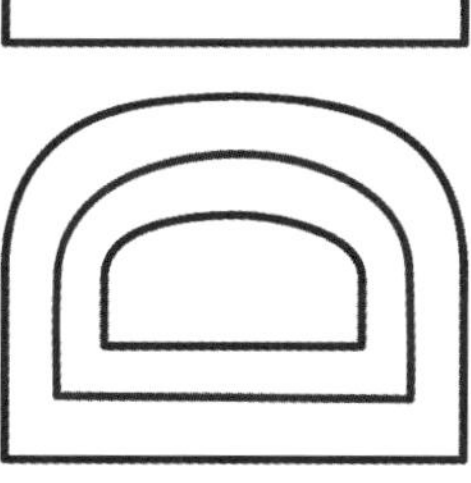

Bloom Hoop Page 98
100% Actual size 152.4mm x 152.4mm

Wild Hoop Page 114
100% Actual size 127mm x 127mm

Happy Little Accidents Hoop Page 106
100%. Actual size 177.8mm x 177.8mm

Simple Stitched Placemats Page 56
Actual size
177.8mm x 177.8mm

Chained feather

Cable

Closed Buttonhole

Whipped Backstitch

Cretan

Split

Buttonhole

Polaroid Hoop Page 84

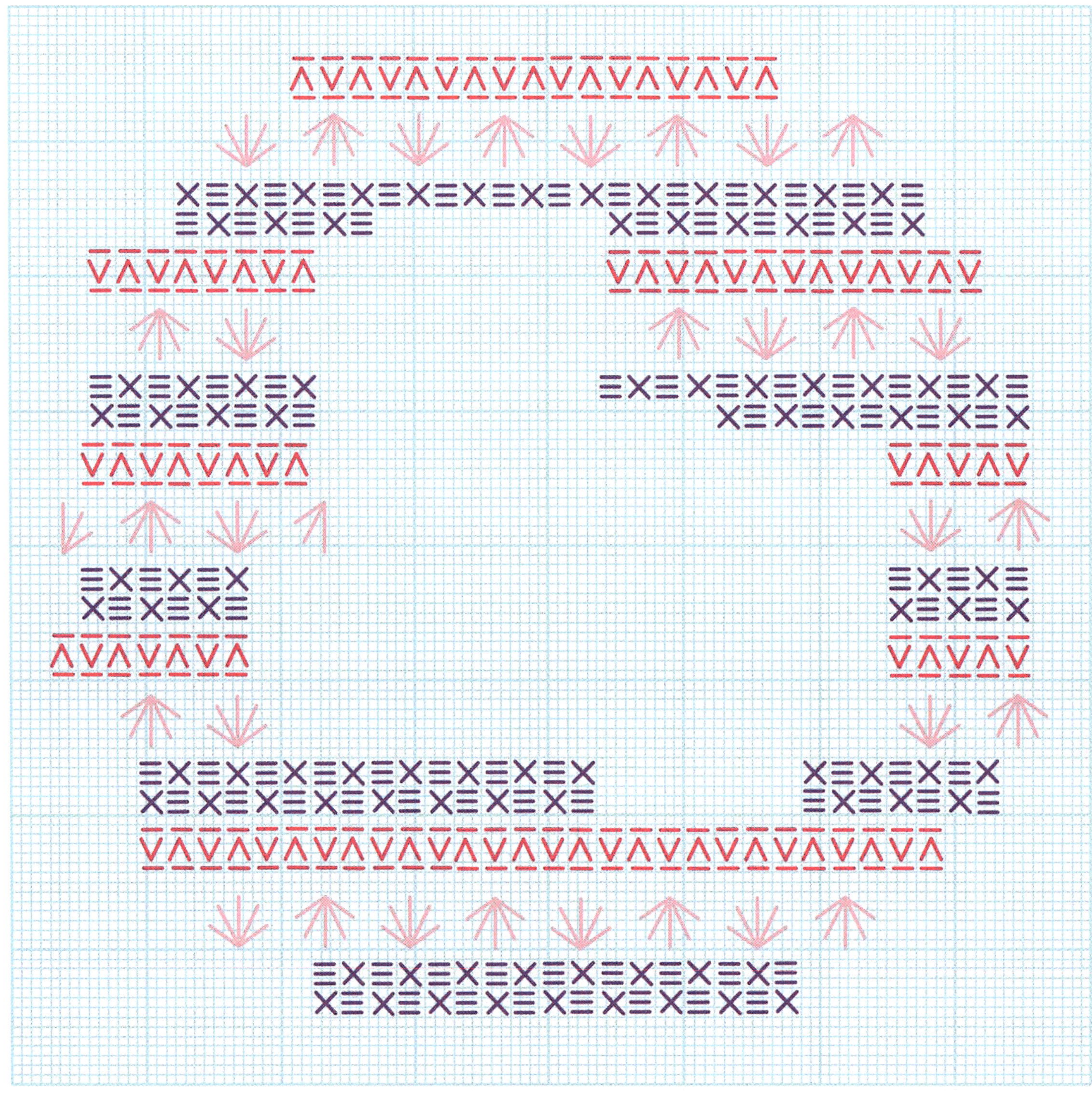

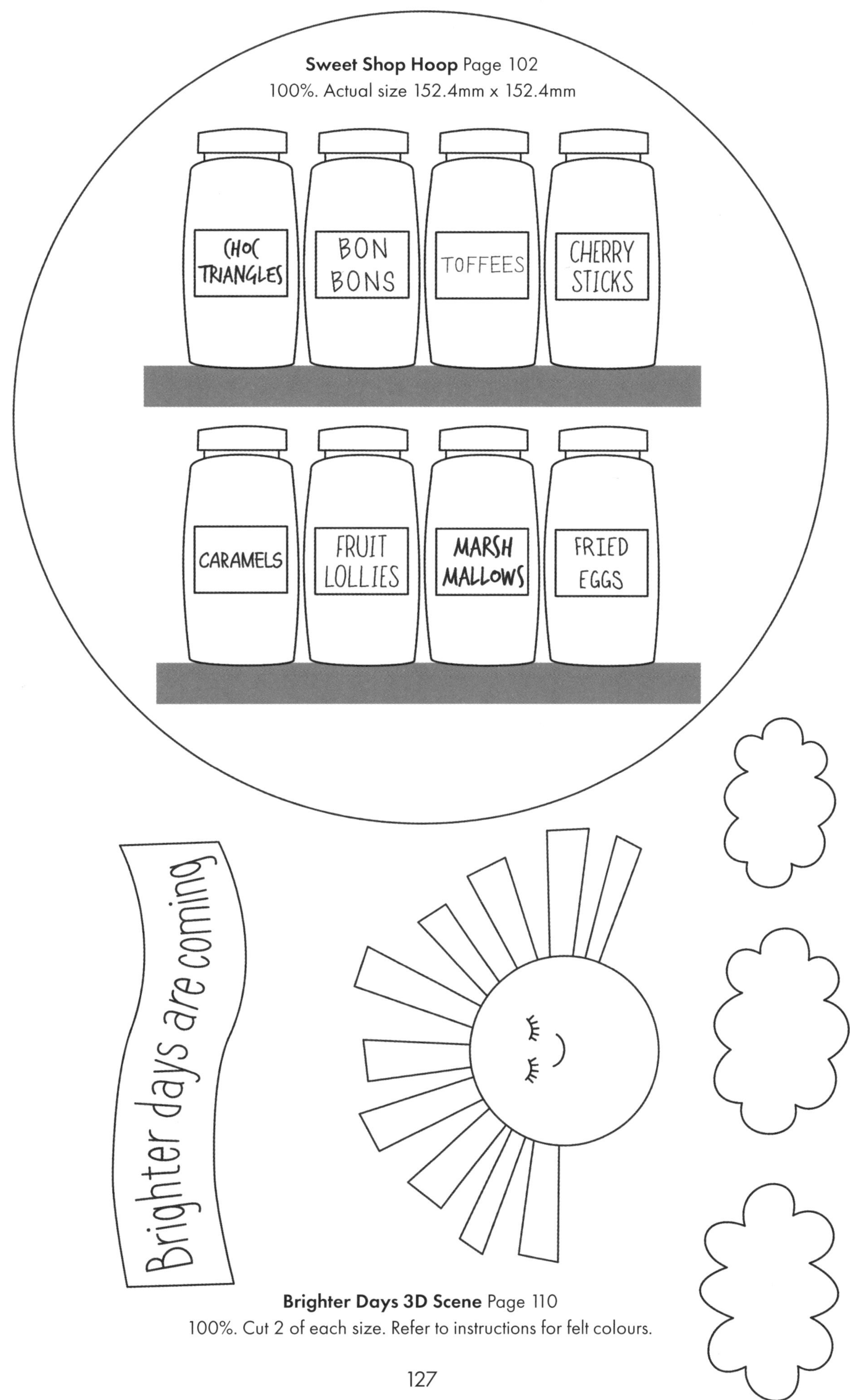

Sweet Shop Hoop Page 102
100%. Actual size 152.4mm x 152.4mm

Brighter Days 3D Scene Page 110
100%. Cut 2 of each size. Refer to instructions for felt colours.

About the author

Clare Albans is a mama, maker and author based in Newcastle upon Tyne. Her brand, Hello! Hooray! is all about taking time out to be creative. Clare creates colourful and modern embroidery designs, writes a blog and runs a curated online haberdashery shop on her website. Her work is inspired by colours and patterns, and features positive words and phrases that are a joy to stitch. An emphasis on enjoying the process of stitching and creating has always been a key mission for her work, and it was a theme throughout her first book, Colourful Fun Embroidery. Clare's work has been featured in many craft publications, and she is a regular contributor to Love Embroidery magazine. Clare juggles her business around home educating her two little ones (who are 7 and 4) with her husband Tom. Their home is a very creative one, and they spend lots of time drawing, painting, baking, making music and getting out and about in and around Newcastle upon Tyne. Clare loves trying out new crafts when she has a spare moment, and is currently experimenting with punch needle embroidery, usually with a cup of tea in hand!
www.hellohooray.com

Acknowledgements

It has been a real privilege to work on my second book, and I am so grateful to so many people for their support during this process. There has been a lot going on behind the scenes whilst writing this book, and it hasn't been an easy journey.

To my husband, Tom, I absolutely could not have done this without you. Thank you for putting your faith in me and encouraging me to follow my dreams no matter what, even when they don't work out.

My children, Evie and Alfie, you are beautiful, amazing humans and you make me so proud every day. I hope you will always follow your dreams - remember that you can do anything!

My family have been brilliant and I'm so thankful for you all - Mum, Dad, Keith, Naomi and Ant, thank you so much for all your support.

To my wonderful friends: Daria, Louise, Susie, Amy and Tiffany, who are always ruffling their pom poms for me and cheering me on. I appreciate your words of encouragement, cups of tea and shoulders to cry on. You are the best! A huge thanks to Tina for taking on my old studio - you are a reminder that there are kind humans in this world, and I wish you and all the Totally Polished girls every success. Big love to you all.

To Katherine, Jane, Jesse and everyone at White Owl. You are an amazing team and it is a joy to work with you all.